Toys From American Childhood
1845-1945

Toys From American Childhood
1845-1945

by Tim Luke

Portfolio Press

To purchase additional copies of this book, please contact:
Portfolio Press, 130 Wineow Street, Cumberland, MD 21502
877-737-1200

Library of Congress Catalog Card Number 00-135255
ISBN 0-942620-44-5

Project Editor: Krystyna Poray Goddu
Design and Production: Tammy S. Blank
Cover design by John Vanden-Heuvel Design

Cover photos: Ideal 1906 teddy bear courtesy of Dee Hockenberry; Izannah Walker doll courtesy of Sothebys, Inc.;
Bing locomotive, Hubley Yellow Cab, George Brown Doctor's Buggy and Bliss dollhouse all courtesy of Bertoia
Auctions. Back cover photo courtesy of Tim's Toy Times, Inc.

Printed and bound in Korea

DEDICATION

This book is dedicated to collectors who still play with their toys.

ACKNOWLEDGEMENTS

This book would not have been possible without the overwhelming influences of my family and friends from whom I draw my strength. A special thank you to my parents for their constant support; they first provided me with a wonderful environment to play in as a young child. And I am grateful for the never-ending love, encouragement and unconditional support of my partner, Greg—we did it. Thank you!!

A sincere debt of gratitude goes to Bill and Jeannie Bertoia of Bertoia Auctions for their continued support, and for the use of their extensive photographic library, without which this project never would have materialized.

CONTENTS

FOREWORD

by Krystyna Poray Goddu

"The history of toy-making through the ages is itself like some gigantic and bewitching jigsaw puzzle from which each succeeding writer may choose his handful of pieces and make a different picture," wrote the late English toy scholar Mary Hillier in her 1966 book, *Pageant of Toys*. In *Toys from American Childhood: 1845-1945*, expert Tim Luke has chosen to put together the picture of one important century of toy-making history as he chronicles the one hundred years that revolutionized the field.

This book's title reflects its scope: toys that were a part of American children's lives during that hundred-year period, regardless of their place of origin. Organizing them by their makers, Mr. Luke explores these toys from many points of view: technological, sociological, psychological, historical and, in some cases, most importantly of all, from the creative impulse that served as a toy's inspiration. His is a broad view that looks at each toy individually, rather than a narrow one that attempts to fit a toy's history into any particular theory of his own.

Tim Luke has been an energetic presence in the toy world over the past decade. From his early days at Christie's auction house in New York, where he eventually became a vice-president and head of the department of collectibles, to his life today as a widely traveled auctioneer, appraiser and author, he has infused the field of antique toys with enthusiasm and personality. Readers who have seen him on the PBS television show *Antiques Roadshow* or watched him conduct an auction have witnessed his engaging presentations. His infectious love for his subject crosses many lines to encompass the creators, the children and the collectors as well as the times and trends these toys reflect. Mr. Luke's appreciation of what toys mean to all those whose lives they touch informs his research and his writing.

As a key participant in the booming field of toy collecting over the past decade, he has witnessed numerous significant discoveries as well as presided over record-breaking sales. He shares his personal stories of these events in the "behind-the-scenes" sections that accompany some of the toy histories in this book. These present-day tales not only enliven the historical facts, but provide a taste of the contemporary field of toy collecting.

Preparing this book with Mr. Luke has been an always rewarding, though occasionally frustrating, challenge. From our earliest discussions in 1997 to the final days of proofreading in 2000, the process has been filled not only with a continuous accumulation of knowledge, but with a deepening appreciation for the toys, their creators and the times from which they emerged. As a writer and editor since 1981, I have done extensive research on dolls and teddy bears, but many of the other toys in this book were new to me. Editing a book is always an opportunity to learn more about a subject, but never have I faced such a vast subject with such a dearth of documented sources. The many contradictory facts, dates and credits make this a difficult field to research. It is the rare toy company that kept records and samples. Researching often means documenting through advertisements in trade and general publications, and seeking out company catalogs or order forms. You must have the thrill of the search to be successful, as well as a dogged persistence to uncover and match up conflicting facts, and a capacity for making assumptions based on the context of the information's presentation. Facts as basic as a toy company's official name, or its actual dates of founding and dissolution, can be difficult to verify.

While distinguished toy scholars such as Mary Hillier, or the American Blair Whitton and, in dolls, the Coleman family, have done a great deal to advance our knowledge of antique toys, the field has simply not had its due as a subject of serious study. I hope that our book will take a major step towards filling that gap. For in spite of the more than thirty books in the bibliography, there is no one book that accomplishes what we have set out to do: to pinpoint and study the major toy makers that played a significant role in American children's lives from the middle of the nineteenth to the middle of the twentieth centuries.

The eighty-six companies profiled in this book produced the toys that filled American children's days with delight. Simply reciting their names conjures up a well of memories for the adults who once were those children. Some of these names live on today; some of these companies are still making toys. Occasionally they are still led by the descendants of the original toy makers, as at the Gund company in New Jersey, where Jacob Swedlin's grandson, Bruce Raiffe, presides over the production of stuffed toys, following in his parents' and grandparent's footsteps. And what American child today has not played with a Fisher-Price toy? Other of these names, such as Charles Crandall and J. & E. Stevens, are virtually unknown to children and parents today, though in their time they were important innovators.

Some of the most compelling stories told here are those of individuals whose strong personal visions found expression in the creation of toys. The fascinating story of the German doll maker Käthe Kruse and her unorthodox life is as much a page-turner as any current best-seller; Louis Marx's immensely successful company was driven by his early ambition to bring mass-production to toy manufacturing. Beatrice Alexander, Milton Bradley and Alfred Gilbert were all founders of toy empires rooted in their personal goals and interests. Yet other companies are barely known by their names; rather they are famous solely for their universally loved creations. What child could identify Georgene Novelties or Duncan? Yet mention Raggedy Ann or yo-yos and their eyes light up.

We have tried to give each company the pages it deserves for recognition, but achieving such a balance is always difficult. Companies that are amply discussed in other sources are sometimes given less space here, in favor of providing information that can not be found elsewhere. And it must be admitted that however much one tries to be unbiased, the author's and editor's personal interests cannot help but bear some weight. Readers will also note that while the book focuses on a particular period, more recent pieces are occasionally shown in an attempt to provide some aid in distinguishing a company's earlier and later production.

Of course there are always gaps. We began with eighty companies, and continued to add not only additional photos as we found them, but additional companies until the very last days of preparing this book for publication. In the end, there must be an ending. A book must be published to fulfill its purpose.

Finally, we could not leave out the children. It was simply not right to publish a book about toys without showing them in their most vital context: with children. In earlier centuries, children's portraits often showed the child with a favorite plaything. So, too, in the early days of photography, children were often posed with toys in formal portraits. While these photographs hardly represent the imaginative pleasures toys provided their owners, they do remind us that at the beginning and at the end, toys are meant for a child's play. We chose to frame these histories with vintage photographs that serve as such reminders.

It is humbling to remember, too, however, that regardless of our enthusiasm for these playthings, or our successes and failures in identifying them, "the toys remain," as Mary Hillier wrote. Products of an individual's imagination and the ensuing work of a team of artisans, the objects have a physical life and presence. Artifacts from earlier eras, they harbor the stories both of their creators and of their playmates. Long after the children who played with them, and their memories, have grown silent, the toys live on.

INTRODUCTION

When I was growing up in the 1960s, I always waited eagerly for Christmas, when I could count on receiving the latest toy that was all the rage. I never noticed the manufacturer or the history of the toy maker, or took into account the calculated increase in "value potential" that the new toy might provide in the future. I and most of the other kids in the neighborhood lived for the day, playing with our Tonka dump trucks, setting up miles of Hot Wheel tracks or competing at Monopoly on rainy days. I remember my army of G.I. Joes capturing my sister's Barbie, taking her prisoner and forcing the fashion queen to jump out of the second-floor window. Toys seemed to dominate my life. Toys gave me the power to transform my life and become a fireman, or a racecar driver, then plan entire housing developments complete with roads, bridges and highways. Many of the toys from my childhood (as well as those from earlier eras) would be banned today for safety issues, but these toys helped stimulate the imagination and foster socialization of kids around the world. I can remember gathering up the kids in the neighborhood with all of

our tractors and cars to construct huge cities. There were Lincoln Log houses in the town and Hot Wheel cars on the roads. Before dark, when our moms called us in for dinner, we would say goodnight, knowing we would continue the expansion of the town the next morning.

During the mid-1960s, the manufacturers of these toys— Marx, Mattel, Tonka— never dreamed their mass-produced toys would have any "secondary market value." Toy companies of my childhood, like other toy companies in earlier eras, all wanted their latest creation to become the new fad, the toy no child could live without, thus creating a demand that would clear out the warehouses. The idea of toys' "secondary market value" has only become popular over the past twenty years, as boldly illustrated by Barbies, Cabbage Patch Kids, Beanie Babies and Furbies.

Being the oldest child of three and the first grandchild in the family guaranteed that I would receive an abundance of playthings. The ones that immediately come to mind are Hot Wheel cars with miles of orange track, a Big Wheel, electric HO scale trains, a Tony the Pony riding horse by Marx and a pair of pedal cars. The pedal cars included a black plastic Batmobile and my prized possession, a red Ford Mustang. At the time, Mom and Dad had a 1964 blue Ford Mustang, and I felt so grown-up with my own car. I still remember driving down the freshly paved driveway in that red pedal car Mustang. Years later, while I was working in the collectibles department of Christie's auction house in New York City, assembling a variety of sales of antique toys and collectibles, I came across an article about pedal cars at auction in the Midwest. One of the sale's highlights was a red Ford Mustang from the 1960s, which had sold for $25,000. My first reaction was to call my parents and see if they might still have the car hidden in the attic. To my disappointment and theirs, the toy had been played with, left in the rain, rusted and put to rest at the local dump years ago. That was the first time that I experienced the strong nostalgic tug of a toy that makes it such a powerful collectible. I was twenty-eight years old, and to have something from my childhood reach "collectible" status gave me a unique feeling. It also gave me a better perspective on toys made one hundred years ago, and a better understanding of the secondary market of collectibles. It illustrated all too clearly how strongly memories are linked with objects. When we see an important object from our past, it triggers the "Oh my God, I had one of those!" response. Nostalgia is a driving force in the collectibles industry today. The histories of the companies that produced the toys we loved in our past contribute to the legacies of the objects we cherish as collectors.

During my tenure at Christie's I was exposed to some of the biggest and best collections in the world. I met outgoing, informed collectors who offered their opinions on all the items being prepared for auction, and others who were just starting out collecting toys, who needed to be educated on the subject. In doing my research for the different auctions, I discovered that the world of toy collecting is made up of a vast number of companies from around the globe—designers, manufacturers, distributors—as well as of cir-

cumstances that have shaped and affected the market over the years. The company histories always fascinated me, especially the stories of the men and women who were passionate about their convictions and their business and were able to overcome the odds, the criticisms, the lack of financing and continue to strive for their goals. This book focuses on the stories of the people behind the toy companies and provides information on the toys they created.

As an auctioneer of toys and collectibles, I have come upon many items that displayed varying degrees of rarity, and even caused a stir in the collectibles world. Two events remain especially vivid in my mind. The first was the December 10, 1991, bankruptcy auction at Christie's of the Mint and Boxed store and warehouse, which provided collectors the opportunity to see and bid on some of the rarest and finest toys in the world. It was at this auction that an early American tinplate hose reel fire toy made by George Brown sold for $231,000, achieving a world record for a tin toy at auction. The second event occurred during a Bill Bertoia auction on May 2, 1998 of the Stanley P. Sax Collection of Mechanical Banks. This collection represent-

ed the "holy grail" to bank collectors. Of particular importance was Lot 151: the Old Woman In The Shoe cast-iron mechanical bank. This example was one of only two known to exist. I opened the bidding at $100,000 and did not stop until the gavel came down at $426,000! Another world record—for a mechanical bank at auction—was set. The sale in its entirety consisted of 251 lots, and totaled over five million dollars.

Stories like these have become an exciting part of the toy collecting scene, and I will share some of them with you in the "behind-the- scenes" sections throughout this book. It is important, however, that we never lose sight of the heart of toy collecting: the love of play and the appreciation of craftsmanship that enhances our joy in playthings.

AN OVERVIEW OF THE HISTORY OF TOYS

The concept of toys is nearly as old as civilization itself. Playthings have been found in ancient tombs in Egypt. Fragile hand-crafted wooden animals, dolls and even simple mechanical toys and board games have been found during archeological digs. Because the Egyptians filled tombs for the dead with items they might need in the next life, it is hard to determine if the artifacts were ceremonial or meant for children's play. During the reign of the Roman Empire, children played with marbles made of fired clay, stone or glass, and had rag dolls similar to the ones we see today. Since the concept of playthings has been with us for so many generations, could this account for the overwhelming popularity of toys in the collectibles market? On some subconscious level, we all find a certain comfort and delight in toys. Toys have been a universally recognized aspect of nearly every culture throughout time.

The period in history after the fall of the Roman Empire is referred to as the "Dark Ages." Very few advances in technology, science or culture took place. Since toys are a direct reflection of a society and a time period it stands to reason that during such an age there would be very few advances in playthings. It was not until the late sixteenth century that the seeds of the toy industry took root.

The ideal location for the growth of a toy industry at that time was a well-traveled trade route with access and distribution throughout Europe, and an abundance of guilds and craftsmen in the area. During the fifteenth century, Nuremberg, Germany, had established itself as a major stop on the trade routes around Europe. There were many guilds manufacturing utensils, religious articles and other household items. Eventually, peasants in the neighboring regions of Germany began to carve a few toys, which agents from Nuremberg collected for sale in the city. As the market for these carved wooden toys grew, so did the network of families involved in their production. Some carvers spent their entire lives carving two or three examples that had become popular in the rest of the world. This is how the cottage industry of toy production was born. For the next two hundred years this industry continued to flourish. The materials used in the production of toys expanded to include wood, paper, cardboard, leather and, by the late 1700s, silver and tinplate.

The sixteenth and seventeenth centuries were a time of constant geographical change. The American colonies were settled in the first quarter of the eighteenth century, but in the early 1700s most manufactured goods were still being imported from England. One of the first industries in the New World was printing, which grew from publishing newspapers to printing inexpensive board games, cards and other material for both adults and children. One early American game, *Lottery of the Pious* or the *Spiritual Treasure Casket* was printed in 1744. Most of these early games reflected the strict moral and religious themes associated with the time period.

As the world order changed, the mobility of families increased. The colonies continued to grow as more Europeans set out for the New World to make their claim to land, prosperity and freedom. The growth of the New World culminated in the Revolutionary War, after which the colonists had to prove not only that they could be free, but also that they could be self-sufficient. This meant foundries and craftsmen had to rely more heavily on the materials in the New World to manufacture goods. A currency system was established, factories were set up to manufacture household items and furniture, and before long the United States was recognized in the international community.

At the beginning of the nineteenth century, the German cottage industry of carved wooden toys was slowly being phased out, due in part to the lack of reforestation over the centuries and the advances in the manufacturing techniques of mass-production. By the 1840s, these innovations included the stamping of tinplate, molding of papier-mâché and iron casting, which revolutionized the industry of toy manufacturing. No longer did an entire toy have to be made by hand. In America, there were a few manufacturers that produced toys, though on a very small scale in comparison to their European counterparts. Later in the nineteenth century, history again affected the overall production of toys in America. The Northern and Southern states had declared a Civil War, and foundries up and down the Atlantic—and particularly in New England—were established to meet the demand for military supplies and ammunition.

Once the war was over, there was no need for the vast production of military supplies. The factories and foundries that had been built now needed something to manufacture. Some turned to basic household items; others turned to toys. During this time period—which was basically the dawn of the Industrial Revolution—some of the most sought-after early American tinplate and cast-iron toys were produced. Wind-up clockwork mechanisms, used in watches, were also placed in tin toys to add movement to the item. The method of sand casting in the production of cast-iron toys was perfected. The early toy manufacturers were also artisans, who perfected their craft and added hand-painted details to mass-produced products. Bell toys, still banks, horse-drawn fire engines, and mechanical banks are just a few examples of the cast-iron craftsmanship and artistry of the day, which reached its pinnacle in America. The European community had been using iron for parts, wheels and other structural supports, but never quite appreciated the versatility of the substance like the American craftsmen. The English produced a few cast-iron mechanical banks, but could not duplicate the sand-casting techniques used in America. American craftsmen cornered the market when it came to both quality and quantity of cast-iron toys.

While the Americans worked with the sand-casting techniques, the Germans and other European companies were mass-producing tinplate toys and perfecting the lithographic process so as to add color to the designs of their toys. Most popular during this period were the wind-up toys that had stamped tinplate gears, rather than the heavy brass clockwork mechanisms found in early American toys. Stamped tinplate gears gave the toy a lighter feel and faster movement. European toy production became entirely mechanized. From whirling tops to trains and trolleys, everything produced had its own locomotion and was colorfully lithographed. The German companies of Lehmann, Bing and Märklin established themselves as leaders in the industry. They exported toys around the world, and it has been estimated that by 1900 nearly one-third of all tinplate toys manufactured in Germany were sold in the United States.

Once again history intervened to establish the toy industry as one of the cornerstones of American ingenuity and craftsmanship in the field of manufacturing. At the end of the nineteenth century the American economy was booming. Entire families worked twelve-hour days to meet the manufacturing demand. Children as young as five and six years of age were put to work. A lack of supervision resulted in numerous maimings and accidental deaths, which in turn brought about reform of labor practices. Children were no longer allowed to work in the factories and found themselves with an abundance of free time and the need for entertainment.

Children in the Victorian era were provided with games and toys that not only entertained, but also educated. Mechanical banks were great fun, but also taught the children the lesson of being thrifty. Toys were manufactured to illustrate Bible characters like Jonah and the Whale, or to depict newspaper cartoon characters of the time like Little Nemo and fairy-tale characters like Mother Goose.

The 1890s showcased the talents of inventors around the world. The times were exciting and innovations were quickly changing the economic and social landscape of the world. Cities around the United States and the world were feeling the effects of the automobile and electric power. No longer would the horse and carriage or kerosene lamp be as important. These advances were also duplicated in miniature. Toy automobiles, trains, airplanes and boats were produced to keep up with the new innovations. The advances made in the last decade of the nineteenth century and the first decade of the twentieth helped shape the future of the twentieth century, while making obsolete the previous years of technology and inventions.

In America, the early 1900s witnessed the use of pressed steel in the production of sturdy trucks, tractors and trains. Steel and tinplate toys gave way to composition, which gave the toy the appearance of wood, but was cheaper and easier to use. Composition consisted of wood chips, pulp, sawdust and leftover materials all mixed with glue and pressed together. Composition itself soon gave way to rubber and celluloid. Every new breakthrough material brought with it the promise of a bigger and better item that was more durable or more efficient. Steam and electricity were harnessed for use in trains, and by the middle of the century, battery-operated playthings dominated toy production.

The 1960s stimulated our appetite for space exploration and all things futuristic. The toy market responded with battery-operated and wind-up robots, space ships and other space-age vehicles. Materials such as plastics, tin, batteries, rubber and steel are still used today; however, digital and virtual-reality games pervade the toy market at the beginning of the twenty-first century.

Historians tell us that history has a way of repeating itself. More than one hundred years ago we experienced social and technological revolutions; the advances and discoveries of the 1990s through 2000 are also redefining the world as we know it. The materials for making toys continue to change. The connection of the global collecting community on the internet is greatly affecting the markets by providing equal access to material, and allowing interested parties anywhere in the world to add to their collections. No longer are antique shops, shows or live auctions the only arena for acquiring pieces. We live in changing times, which present the challenge to continue to grow as collectors. Do not become dormant or content with the status quo or refuse to embark on the journey into the new age of collecting...you will be left behind. Remember the dire predictions for radio and then television. The computer is here to stay and is already becoming an integral part of our everyday life.

This book focuses primarily on companies and toys important in this country in the nineteenth and early twentieth centuries, which helped shape the state of the market today. While many of the companies are American, it was the increasing demand for toys in this country that helped to establish companies in other countries such as the Käthe Kruse doll company, Steiff and Märklin in Germany. This demand also gave rise to American toy companies like Marx, Buddy L, and Lionel. Walt Disney—thanks in particular to Mickey Mouse—must be credited with keeping more than a dozen companies in business during the Depression years of the early 1930s.

The company profiles present both a brief history of the formation and development of each firm, as well as an understanding of the type of toys they produced, and what collectors should look for in their pieces. This book highlights eighty-six popular companies that either produced toys in the United States or exported them here in significant numbers. All of the toys in this book are toys that helped to shape American childhood between 1845 and 1945. As popular playthings for American children during that time, these are the toys that may turn up at local garage sales or flea markets, as well as at antiques shows and auction.

Entire books exist devoted to specific areas of toy collecting, and even to some of the individual companies included here. My purpose in this book is to provide a condensed look at eighty-six toy companies, often highlighting key individuals at these companies and examining how their vision affected the direction of toy design and manufacture. Each profile is accompanied by as many examples as possible of the toys manufactured by the company, as well as by identification clues and collector alerts, wherever possible. My hope is that the illustrations and identification aids will help collectors identify and understand their pieces, and that the histories will inspire, enlighten and deepen our appreciation for these treasures of childhoods past.

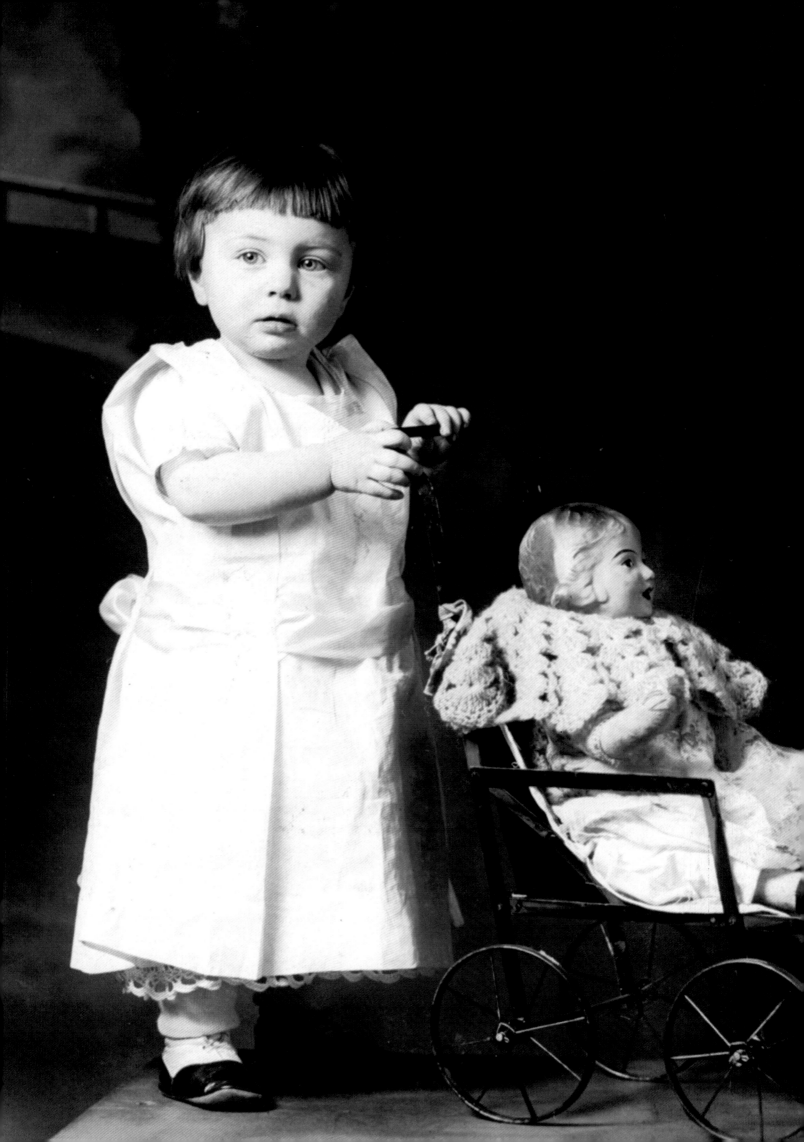

THE TOY MAKERS

Alexander Doll Company
New York, New York
1923

Identification Clues

- Dolls are usually marked ALEXANDER on the back of the doll or at the hairline at the back of the neck

- Clothes are marked with white label with blue lettering MADAME ALEXANDER

Beatrice Alexander Behrman, the daughter of Russian and Austrian immigrants, founded this legendary American doll company that is still in operation today. Beatrice was born Bertha Alexander in New York City on March 9, 1895. As a child, she helped her stepfather, Maurice Alexander, who established and operated New York's first doll hospital, with repairs and reconstruction. She observed the joy a doll could bring to a young child, and also witnessed the tears when a doll was brought in for repair. In 1912, she married Phillip Behrman and three years later their only child, Mildred, was born. Alexander first experimented with making cloth dolls with her sisters, during the toy shortages of World War I, and continued to perfect her skills in the years following. In 1923, she officially created the Alexander Doll Company. She soon became known as Madame Alexander or, simply, Madame. Her dolls are often referred to as Madame Alexander dolls.

By the early 1930s Alexander had a production facility to manufacture her designs. Her cloth creations, which had mohair wigs, molded-mask faces of felt or flocked fabric, sewn-on limbs and painted eyes, included Alice in Wonderland and the Little Women characters as well as other literary figures. She hit a gold mine when she had the idea to buy the license to repro-

duce the famous Dionne Quintuplets as dolls in 1935; the company produced them in cloth and then later in composition—a material consisting of wood pulp, glue, sawdust, flour, rags, and a variety of other substances.

In the 1930s the Alexander Doll Company produced primarily composition dolls; Madame followed up the success of the Dionne Quintuplets by reproducing the young Princess Elizabeth and Margaret Mitchell's heroine Scarlett O'Hara—which she released with the premiere of the film, *Gone with The Wind*—as dolls, and then Snow White, timed to appear on store shelves when the first feature-length cartoon film appeared in movie theatres. In 1936 *Fortune* magazine featured Madame Alexander, along with Effanbee and Ideal, as the three major American dollmakers of the era.

After World War II, Madame continued to be a pioneer in doll-making, as she became the first manufacturer to make use of the new medium of hard plastic for her dolls. Madame Alexander's perseverance and creativity were rewarded by recognition and many awards for the company's doll designs, both during her lifetime and after her death in 1990. Still actively producing dolls today, the Alexander Doll Company is one of the best-known American doll companies of the twentieth century.

Behind The Scenes

While I was conducting an appraisal event at the Winterthur Museum in Delaware, a young women named Karen came up to the table with three dolls in their original boxes and was curious to see if they were of any value. During our conversation I discovered Karen had bought an old house, including all the contents from attic to basement, that had belonged to her great-aunt. Karen and her husband needed to sell or throw out the items they did not want. While going through the attic, Karen came across the Alexander dolls.

By the looks of the dolls, it appeared her aunt had never played with them. The dresses were in fantastic condition, and the dolls themselves looked like new. Even the boxes containing the dolls, which are usually discarded or deteriorated, were in excellent condition.

My preliminary evaluation was based on the fresh look of the dolls and their boxes, so I informed Karen that her Winnie Walker Doll and Polly Pigtails could each bring $250-$350 at auction. Karen consigned them to my internet auction gallery, TreasureQuest Auction Gallery, Inc., and within an hour of posting the item on the internet, we had e-mail questions and bids on the dolls. The final selling price? Polly Pigtails brought $550, and Winnie Walker was sold for more than $400. Not bad for an attic find.

Opposite page: In 1935 Madame Alexander first produced a set of 8-inch composition Dionne Quintuplets in a stroller. She also produced a set of 16-inch cloth Quintuplets in 1935. For many years, the Alexander boxes featured a photo of Madame. **This page, top:** Among the many storybook characters the Alexander company produced was McGuffey Ana. These three 16-inch composition examples date from 1937-1944. **Left:** Composition fairy-tale characters by the Alexander Doll Company included, from left, Snow White, 13 inches, and Dopey, 12 inches, in 1938, and an 8-inch Dopey marionette designed by puppeteer Tony Sarg in 1936.

Above: As the Dionne Quintuplets grew, the Alexander Doll Company's dolls aged with them. In 1937 the famous two-year-olds were recreated as 11-inch composition dolls. **From left** they are: Yvonne, Cecile, Annette, Marie and Emilie. **Right:** Among Madame Alexander's very earliest dolls were depictions of Louisa May Alcott's *Little Women*. This set of 16-inch cloth dolls dates somewhere between 1930-36.

Above: When King George VI was crowned in 1937, the Alexander Doll Company immortalized the young monarch-to-be, his daughter Princess Elizabeth, as a 13-inch composition doll. **Left:** Composition baby dolls made by the company include, **left**, Pinky Baby, 20 inches, circa 1937 and Slumbermate, 14 inches, circa 1940. Both have cloth bodies.

Above: These cloth dolls by the Alexander Doll Company were inspired by characters from children's books. From left, they are: Kate Greenaway, 16 inches, 1936-38; Little Shaver, 22 inches, 1940; Little Lord Fauntleroy, 16 inches, 1932; and Little Shaver, 7 inches, 1940-44. **Right:** The Alexander Doll Company produced these composition 12-inch-high Twins in 1936.

Althof, Bergman & Company
New York, New York
1867 - 1880

This early American toy manufacturer became an innovator in children's playthings when it incorporated a clockwork mechanism into the design of its toys. The growing need for children's toys provided the impetus for the three Bergman brothers to join forces with a partner, L. Althof, to form their company in New York City in 1867. The company is credited with manufacturing some of the best known and most sought-after tinplate creations. The company distinguished itself as one of the first American companies to produce tinplate floor trains, hoop toys, still banks and horse-drawn vehicles. This company also took pride in the artistry behind every painted clockwork toy manufactured. Among other playthings in their production line were bell toys; boats; fire engines; and miniature kitchen and household furniture for dollhouses.

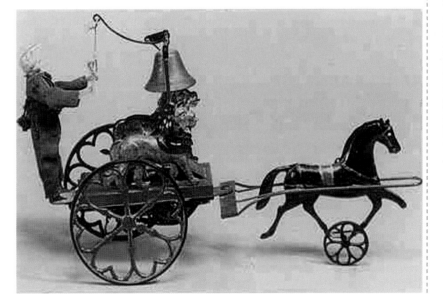

Top: This tinplate floor toy is a fine example of this company's craftsmanship. **Above:** This bell toy illustrates the common use of animals as themes in toys of this period. **Left:** This rare May Queen horse-drawn bell toy features the elaborate cast-iron wheel design combined with delicate hand-painted tinplate animals and a bisque-headed figure of a girl.

American Flyer
Chicago, Illinois
1907 - 1966

Identification Clues

• Train cars and locomotives are usually marked with company name

• Some cars and locomotives appear to be of lesser quality than Lionel trains

• Lightweight material and low quality paint or lithography

William Hafner of Chicago, Illinois, decided to venture into the toy manufacturing business early in the twentieth century. At first, he concentrated on clockwork automobiles. During the transitions of the new century, as society changed, Hafner's creations reflected all the advances in technology. Clockwork mechanisms became the consistent component in all the pieces manufactured.

As the company struggled internally with production and distribution of their products, the name was changed from the Toy Auto Company to the W. F. Hafner Company. As the industrial revolution began to make its mark on the American economy, it also affected the production of Hafner's toys. When the locomotive joined the east and west coasts, transportation and cargo shipments by train became more popular. Hafner, facing financial difficulty, entered into a partnership with William Coleman, a Chicago hardware storeowner. In 1910, they decided to produce clockwork trains and the company once again

changed names, to its final moniker, American Flyer. Four years later, Hafner formed a rival company called Overland Flyer to compete with his original company.

Eventually American Flyer was experimenting with different products to compete with other manufacturers. In addition to the successful train line, the company designed four different styles of mechanical airplanes: the Spirit of Columbia, Lone Eagle, Spirit of America and Sky King. Production of these airplanes lasted only from 1928 to 1931. The company dropped the airplanes from the line and focused on the production of trains, establishing itself as one of the leaders in the toy train markets. They produced their popular line through the mid 1930s. In 1938, the company was bought by the A.C. Gilbert Company, which is best known for erector sets. Gilbert made a variety of changes in the American Flyer production of trains. After World War II, the company introduced "S" gauge railroad models that had little success. The Lionel Company bought out American Flyer in 1966.

Collector Alert

Look for the best quality and condition you can find. Most of these trains were made of a lesser-quality material than Lionel trains and therefore damage easily.

Opposite page, top, and this page, above: American Flyer manufactured many passenger sets like these two examples. **Opposite page and this page, top:** Advertisements for American Flyer toys appeared frequently in magazines, and have become popular with collectors today. These advertisements date from December 1925.

Arcade Manufacturing Company
Freeport, Illinois
1885 - 1946

Heralded for its production of cast-iron automotive toys, Arcade used its slogan, "They Look Real," as the foundation for its design concepts. In 1885, the company, an outgrowth of the earlier Novelty Iron & Brass Foundry, established itself in the farming community of Freeport, Illinois. Answering the need for commercial farm equipment and other household necessities, Arcade started producing a variety of items that ranged from feed grinders and plows to coffee grinders and windmills. Toy production followed in 1888 and continued through 1946. Arcade produced trains, banks, stoves and novelties. By 1920,

the company's most famous creation, the yellow cab, was such a large success that a flock of automobile derivatives were created to meet the overwhelming demand for Arcade toys. By the end of the 1930s, more than three hundred different toys were being offered in the company's production line.

Responding to the growing demand for toys of good quality, Arcade also manufactured dollhouse furniture, cast-iron penny toys and toy banks. Most of the twentieth-century Arcade toys have the company name cast right into the toy, which makes for easy identification and dating of the toy.

Identification Clues

• Look for the ARCADE name cast into the toy

• In addition to transportation toys, with a focus on automotive, the company also produced character items like Andy Gump Roadster 348 and Chester Gump in his pony cart

Opposite page and this page: Arcade manufactured a diverse range of cast-iron toys, from airports and service stations to cars and farm vehicles. They were widely advertised in magazines like *Child Life.* The ad shown on the opposite page appeared in that magazine in 1927.

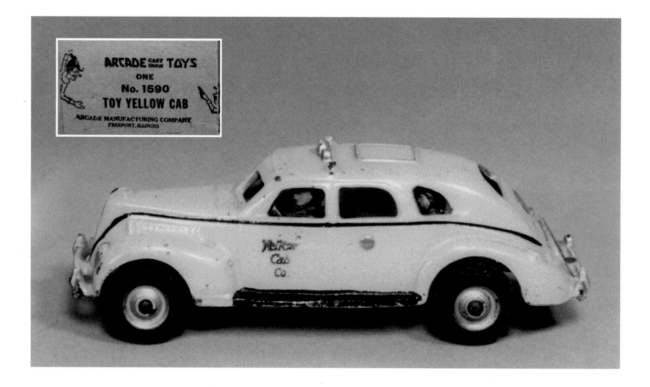

By the end of the 1930s, more than three hundred different toys were offered by Arcade. The company's most famous creation was the yellow cab, above, created before 1920.

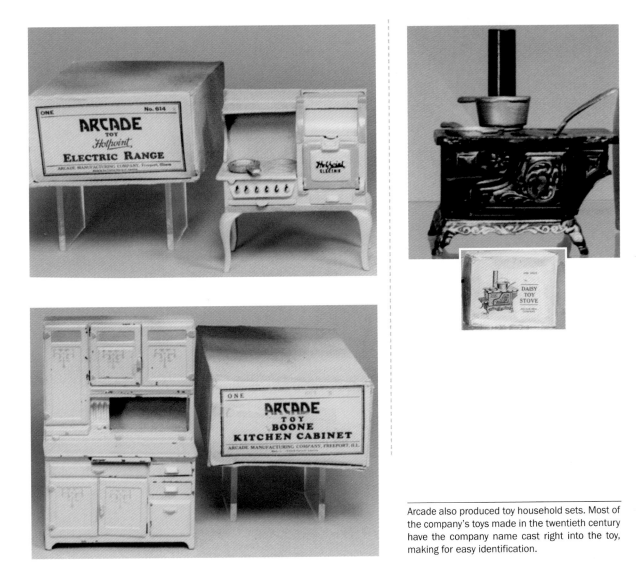

Arcade also produced toy household sets. Most of the company's toys made in the twentieth century have the company name cast right into the toy, making for easy identification.

Barclay Manufacturing Company
Hoboken, New Jersey
1923 - 1971

Barclay produced lead soldiers, measuring approximately 1½ to 3 inches high, in a variety of realistic styles and poses during the 1930s. In 1940, reacting to retailers' complaints about the tin helmets frequently coming off, Barclay moved from slush-casting to die-casting its soldiers with cast helmets, as shown above.

The success of World War I left the American people with a feeling of community that had never before been experienced in this country. In 1923, Leon Donze and Michael Levy established the Barclay Manufacturing Company in New Jersey, and became the largest American producer of toy soldiers. The war provided the most publicity and advertising for the toys. In the 1930s Barclay produced small soldiers, jeeps, and a variety of military vehicles and personnel.

Gebrüder Bing

Nuremberg, Germany
1866 - 1933

Two brothers, Ignaz and Adolf Bing, who started out as tinware dealers in Germany eventually founded a tin toy company. The brothers first distributed household items and toys around 1864. Soon after they had established themselves in the distribution business, they began to work on developing their own toys, and ultimately pioneered mass-production techniques in the development of toys. They became known for the use of superior clockwork mechanisms in their mechanical toys, along with the production process of cutting and shaping metal. They also excelled in, and garnered much attention for, the use of highly detailed and decorated lithographic process on the metal work.

By 1882 the company had a number of successful toy lines that included spring-driven boats, cars and double-decker buses. They also made construction sets, and a phonograph that played three speeds. Their most innovative and popular item was the toy train. As the company continued to prosper and grow they expanded production to include teddy bears. Bing was one of the first to jump on the teddy-bear wagon in 1906, when they made their first teddy, and continued to expand their line of toys by adding elaborate tin ocean liners. The stuffed bears and tin ocean liners all bear the superior craftsmanship and attention to detail that made the toys so popular with children of the era, as well as with collectors today.

Production levels increased and warehouses were filled with stock to keep up with the international level of demand for Bing toys. The company fell into management troubles around 1919, and a business partner, Werke, purchased the company. His contribution also included a new logo that was designed to incorporate the change in ownership. Toys produced from 1919 to 1932 were marked with the new logo of B.W. for Bing-Werke. The American stock market crash of 1929 affected production and halted the creation of new items for distribution. The company began to falter, and in 1932 the increased level of inventory coupled with a lack of buyers forced the company to cease toy production. In 1933 Karl Bub took over the Bing train production while Fleischmann grabbed the toy boat inventory.

Identification Clues

- From the turn of the twentieth century until about 1906 the "GBN" letters were each in a circle enclosed in a diamond outline and crest design

- The logo used from 1906 to 1919 was a metal chip placed in the teddy bears' ears, or an imprint on the tinplate toys of GBN (Gerb. Bing Nuremberg)

- From about 1906 – 1919 the script version of "GBN" enclosed in a circle was used primarily on trains and steam engines

- From 1912 – 1923 the block letters of "GBN" enclosed in a square were used

- From 1923, a small inverted "B" was placed above the "W" to incorporate Werke into the company name and logo

- Bing teddy bears are made from mohair of high quality, usually have excelsior stuffing, glass or shoe-button eyes and are fully jointed

Above: The steam engine locomotive and tender was Bing's most innovative and popular item.

Collector Alert

Look out for repainting or artificially distressed work on trains, boats and automobiles, which devalues the piece. Some steam engines and trains that were used have chipped or missing paint. This is not a problem, provided that other paint was not applied to the piece in an attempt to fix it up.

Opposite page, top and center: The fleet of wind-up Bing ocean liners included luxury vessels along with gunboats. **Left:** The black locomotives are examples of early Bing trains with clockwork mechanism, while the green engine features the logo from a later time period. **This page, top left:** Bing's clockwork gunboat showcases the company's attention to artistry and detail. **Center:** This pair of open touring cars with original Bing figures reflect the popularity of automobiles during this period. **Above:** This 14-inch mohair bear, circa 1915, has no button under its left arm, but displays all the basic characteristics of the company's teddy bears, as does the Bing bear, **top,** which is 20 inches high, circa 1920, and also lacks its button.

The R. Bliss Manufacturing Company
Pawtucket, Rhode Island
1832 - 1914

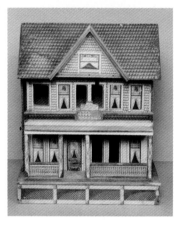

T he Bliss Manufacturing Company was a pioneer and leader in the market of lithographed paper-on-wood toys. Established in 1832 by Rufus Bliss in Pawtucket, Rhode Island, the firm produced a wide variety of wooden toys that ranged from elaborately detailed horse-drawn carriages and trolley cars to architectural blocks, boats and fire toys. The company was able to establish itself as a market leader by producing its toys with the highest level of craftsmanship and detailed accuracy. This can be seen in the trains, trolley cars, boats, and especially in their most popular creations, the ornate Bliss dollhouses.

The company added beautiful floor pull toys to their line; the earliest known advertisements for these date from 1871. Bliss became the first toy company to manufacture a toy telephone set. Throughout the company's history, it continued to improve on the lithographic processes that were colorful and eye-catching to both children and adults. The toy division was sold to Manson & Parker of Winchendon, Massachusetts in 1914, and continued to produce toys through 1935.

Identification Clues

- Ornately designed, lithographed paper on wood

- Simple and accurate representations of boats, trains and carriages of the nineteenth century

- Floor pull toys with grand scale; most items are more than 12 inches in length

Opposite page, top: This paper-on-wood pull toy of a locomotive and train cars amused and educated Victorian children, who played with the blocks that were stored in the train cars. Bottom: It is rare to find a Bliss war ship pull toy with all the flags, masts and cannons intact, like this example. This page, top and above, and opposite page center: Elaborately detailed, lithographed dollhouses were the cornerstone of Bliss's toy line. The three-story example, top, shows the latch on the front door where the front façade would be secured closed, or unlatched to expose the interior. Center: This ornate horse and carriage floor toy has a fairytale theme. Left: Bliss recreated a Union paddleboat as a floor toy.

The R. Bliss Manufacturing Company   39

George Borgfeldt & Company
New York, New York
1881 - 1962

We have this company to thank for the toy-licensing phenomenon that exists today. In 1881, George Borgfeldt formed a partnership with brothers Marcell and Joseph Kahle and created a wholesaler importing business. This new company found its niche in the production and distribution of comic character toys. Borgfeldt & Co. acquired exclusive rights to a variety of manufacturer-copyrighted toys and subcontracted their production to other firms. The toys were then marked with Borgfeldt's "Nifty" logo, a smiling moon face, which became Borgfeldt's trademark.

By the late 1920s cartoon characters in the newspapers were becoming very popular, and Borgfeldt & Co. capitalized on this popularity by snapping up the copyrights to Felix the Cat, Maggie & Jiggs, and Creeping Buttercup. The stable of comic characters in the Borgfeldt domain expanded the business and ensured the success of the company. Continuing to build on earlier success, Borgfeldt looked for other products to import to America. In the late 1930s the company became one of the first American companies to represent the German plush animal manufacturer Margarete Steiff and import her mohair bears to America. Borgfeldt's expertise with comic characters coupled with the high quality of Steiff's toys resulted in a successful collaboration that brought the newly popular comic character Mickey Mouse to life in a plush incarnation.

In addition to comic character toys, Borgfeldt & Co. also commissioned the ever-popular Toonerville Trolley and Highway Henry. These productions were very popular in their day and continue to captivate collectors today. The firm finally closed its doors in 1962.

Collector Alert

When you find these toys in good condition, be sure to do your homework regarding price. I have seen collectors unfamiliar with the market pay three times the market value for a Borgfeldt toy.

Opposite page, top: A long-billed Donald Duck and Homer the Elephant are celluloid characters placed on a simple clockwork wind-up metal trapeeze. The inset features the toy's original box. **Bottom:** Spark Plug and Barney Google were a popular comic character duo, featured here on a lithographed tinplate wind-up toy. **This page: Above left:** Many companies made Mickey Mouse toys that appear to be the same, but note that Borgfeldt's Nifty Drummer, shown on right in photo, with its box in the background, features both the words Jazz Drummer and the company logo on the drum. The other two lithographed tin die-cut Mickey Mouse Drummers are German-made. **Left:** This platform tinplate wind-up toy featuring Felix the Cat uses a simple mechanism, as illustrated in the inset. **Top:** The popular Toonerville Trolley was also used on the wind-up tinplate lithographed toys. **Above:** Maggie and Jiggs were another favorite comic character duo, used here on a tinplate wind-up platform toy.

Milton Bradley

Springfield, Massachusetts
1861

Identification Clues

- Board games and puzzles are dated and marked Milton Bradley
- Look for logo and copyright date and patent to establish the toy's time period
- Early toys are difficult to find because the cardboard or paper deteriorated or was thrown away
- Prices are still affordable in this area of collecting

This company began by making educational toys and maintains that tradition today. The Bradley family can be traced back to 1635 in Salem, Massachusetts. The family tree has roots spread throughout New England, though Milton Bradley himself was born November 8, 1836, in Vienna, Maine. The family stayed in Maine for ten years, then relocated to Lowell, Massachusetts.

In 1856, young Milton Bradley had successfully completed one year at Lawrence Scientific School and was into his second. His classes were challenging; he worked hard at, and took a great interest in, his studies. In the middle of his second year his parents decided to move to Hartford, Connecticut. Unable to support himself and attend school at the same time, Bradley joined his family in Hartford. Work was difficult to find in Hartford, however, he caught word of opportunities in Springfield, Massachusetts, which boasted, at the time, of being the fastest-growing city in New England.

Bradley arrived in Springfield late in 1856 by train, which was his very first exposure to locomotives and the railroads. His first job application to the Wason Car Manufacturing Company, which manufactured railroad engines and cars, brought him success. He was hired on the spot— more for his enthusiasm than for his knowledge of railroad design. He was a quick study and worked for the company on and off for the next four years. In 1860, Bradley was asked by the company to design a special railroad car for the Pasha of Egypt. His design was so spectacular that the company produced a color lithograph of the finished railroad car and presented it to Bradley. That lithograph sparked the flame of what became Bradleyy's lifelong obsession with the lithographic process. He perfected his lithographic technique and printed an extremely popular portrait of a clean-shaven Abraham Lincoln. Sales were very strong until Lincoln decided to grow a beard. This forced Bradley to pursue another direction and led him to finish developing a board game he had started working on a few years earlier.

When "The Checkered Game of Life" was completed, Bradley produced several salesman samples and set out for New York City to place

orders for his new game. The game was so successful that by the end of 1861 he had produced more than forty thousand copies. Adopting the theme of toys that were entertaining and educational, his company produced a kindergarten alphabet set; building blocks featuring numbers and animals; lithographed sheets of paper that could be formed into three-dimensional villages; and its most popular toy, the zoetrope. The zoetrope, also known as the wheel of life, featured a strip of drawings showing figures in the process of an activity. The strip was placed inside a slotted drum that sat atop a pedestal, and could be manually spun. As the drum spun, the figures appeared to be in motion to a viewer peering through the slots. The company continued to grow and produced thousands of puzzles, board and card games and educational construction toys.

These late nineteenth-century games and puzzles illustrate the high quality of lithography that distinguishes Milton Bradley's toys from that era.

William Britains LTD
London, England
1845

Identification Clues

- Lightweight, hollow-cast lead figures

- Hole at the top of the figure's head

- Finely finished figures with great attention to uniform detail

- Figures on horses not removable

- On some figures the only moving part is the sword arm, which goes up and down

This venerable toy manufacturing company began as a family business, with each member contributing to the design and production of the playthings produced. The patriarch of the family, William Britain, possessed the entrepreneurial skills and unshakable faith in the free-enterprise opportunities that presented themselves in Victorian London. The early business of the 1840s centered on the production of simple mechanical tin toys that were manufactured and distributed from his Lambton Road, Hornsey Rise, North London suburban home. Two major factors contributed to the overall success of the business. The first was being blessed with the last name of Britain, which played well within the chauvinistic Victorian English trade; the second was being blessed with a large family of seven boys and girls, who were enthusiastic about their father's ventures and contributed to all aspects of the family business.

The early toys produced by Britains featured clockwork mechanisms that were key- or coin-operated with a sampling that included a walking bear, a Chinese man pulling a rickshaw and a kilted Scotsman who drank a bottle of whisky. The clothed figures had their garments designed, cut and sewn by the female members of the Britain family, while the boys constructed the toys and mechanisms. The family continued to create the tin toys up to World War I, though in smaller quantities as pro-

Above: This pair of boxed Britain sets includes French Foreign Legion No 1711 with five infantry and one mounted officer; Cossacks No 136, with four mounted figures and No. 7301 U.S. Marine Corps featuring four figures. **Right:** Foreign infantry sets were very popular offerings in the company's line. Shown here are the Turkish infantry; Armies of the World; the Polish Infantry; the Japanese Cavalry set; and a pair of Greek Army Evzones sets.

duction of lead soldiers soon took over the focus of the company.

By the 1880s and into the early 1890s, the production of the tin mechanical toys became increasingly more costly which, in turn made them harder to sell. William Britain turned his attention to the marketplace and realized that a number of foreign companies were manufacturing lead soldiers for sale in England. No domestic toy manufacturer was creating the popular figures in the United Kingdom. Noting that foreign manufacturers like Heyde, Mignot, Heinrichsen and Allgeyer dominated the marketplace in the 1890s, Britain decided that it was time to explore the possibility of expanding the scope of the family business to include lead soldiers.

His sons, Alfred and William Jr., helped their father to formulate their plan of attack. They determined that the process used by Heyde in Dresden, Germany, and Mignot in Paris was the best place to start. They used a master model from a military print and created a plaster mold from which a two-piece brass mold was produced and snapped together. When the boiling liquid metal was poured into the mold it would create the lead figure. The brilliant stroke of genius that separated Britains' creations from all the rest occurred one afternoon late in 1892 when William Jr. was under the cherry tree of the garden, experimenting with several pots of boiling metal. William Jr. discovered that by placing tiny air holes at

Above: These two Britains sets of North American mounted Indians still have their original boxes. **Left:** Britain's variety of sets included: French Foreign Legionaires; Cape Town Highlanders; the Argentine Infantry; the Danish Army Life Guard #2019; the Indian Army Service Corps #1893, with six figures and a mule; and the Bersaglieri #169, containing eight figures.

the top of the head of the figure's mold, he could tip some of the molten metal out again in a quick upside-down motion, resulting in the development of the first ever hollow-cast soldier. The secret of the process also relied on the temperature of the metal and the mold, coupled with the speed of the entire process.

It was William's discovery of this process that explains why all the hollow-cast soldiers Britains manufactured have a tiny hole at the top of their head. In the case of the horsemen that were not detachable from their mounts, the lead was poured in through the horse's tail, and there were tiny holes in the horse's nose and the man's head that allowed the air in to release the excess liquid metal. William Jr. perfected his process and in 1893, with the help of his father and siblings, decided to create a model of the Life Guard, the household cavalry of the Queen, that consisted of a mounted figure with fixed arms holding a thin strip of tin for a sword.

The simple creation became a direct competitor to the solid cast-lead soldiers. The hollow-cast pieces

Top: The Railway Station Staff boxed set #1256 includes a station master; ticket collector; porters; passengers; and luggage. Above: The Moutain Gun of the Royal Artillery set includes nine figures; mounted officers; two guns, two cannons and four mules. Right: This grouping of soldiers includes the Abyssinian Tribesman #1425; the British Army Infantry #1544; a regiment of the Belgian Army #2009 and the Belgian Infantry set #189. Original boxes are shown.

were more economical to produce, and thus carried a lower price for the consumer. William's younger brother Fred was elected salesman for the family and he set out to convince the conservative-minded British storeowners that Britains' lead soldiers were worthy of being sold right along with the Heyde and Mignot pieces. After several rejections, Fred finally convinced Albert Gamage, a draper's assistant who opened shop in1878, to carry a small offering of the hollow-cast lead figures in his eclectic rambling bazaar. The success Gamage had with the lead soldiers prompted other storeowners to place orders, and before long the family could hardly keep up with domestic production orders. By the end of the nineteenth century the Britain family had established their company, and the figures they pro-

duced were on every British boy's wish list at Christmas and birthday time.

As time marched on, domestic sales turned into exported international sales. Each World War, minor battle or skirmish around the globe, provided the company with an opportunity to manufacture soldiers that reflected the world events mirrored in hollow-cast lead figures. These were produced with great attention to detail, especially where uniform specificity was concerned. When World War II ended, the production of lead toy soldiers was slow to restart due to the government's restrictions on the use of lead. The only toy soldiers available at this time in the United Kingdom were for export, however, by 1949 normal production had resumed.

Top: This Britains Regiments of All Nations collection includes a French Zouaves set, a Zulus boxed set and the Royal Scots Grey's set, all shown with their original boxes. **Above:** The Boer War period army service set has two horse-drawn supply wagons; ten figures, four seated figures; one mounted officer and four teams of horses mounted by four soldiers. **Left:** This grouping includes six different sets manufactured by Britains: a Camel Corps #123; a mounted Arab set #164; eight Arab figures and there sets featuring the Arabs of the Desert collection.

George W. Brown Company
Forestville. Connecticut
1856 - 1880

This company resulted from the partnership of a clockmaker's apprentice and toy designer, George Brown, and Chauncey Goodrich, a clockmaker. The company became the first manufacturer of American toys to combine clockwork mechanisms with tinplate to produce mechanical toys. The product line was very creative and included boats, vehicles, dancing figures and hoop toys.

The artistry and craftsmanship were reflected in the delicate designs executed on tinplate and metal. The platform toys were produced with intricate detail and this precision also can be seen in their ships, river-boats and dancing figures. The company continued producing toys through 1862, when the company's production line began to alter its focus from playthings to a more practical and popular commodity, brass burners.

In 1868 Brown, wanting to return to his true passion of toy design, sold his company to the Bristol Brass & Clock Company. One year later he and Elisha Stevens of J. & E. Stevens created the Stevens & Brown Manufacturing Company. They continued to produce cast-iron bell toys and a variety of playthings for the next decade. In 1880 the partnership was dissolved.

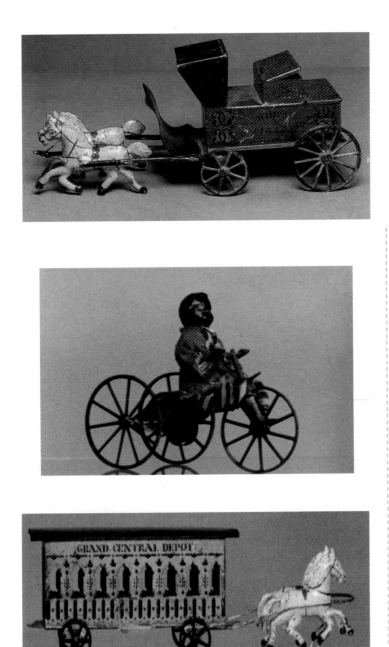

Behind The Scenes

My introduction to the major leagues of the collectible toy auction world came in December 1991, while I was working in the collectibles department at Christie's auction house in New York City. At the time, Christie's had beat out Sotheby's for the opportunity to liquidate the "Mint and Boxed" collection of toys sold on behalf of the trustees in a bankruptcy of the company. The toys from this collection represented some of the best manufacturers in the world, and included some of the only known examples today by certain manufacturers. One such toy was lot 15, "The Charles," the only known example of a tinplate hose reel fire toy by George Brown. It represents American toy craftsmanship and artistry at its finest. The auction room was standing room only, filled with collectors trying to get a piece of the offerings. Since this was a bankruptcy sale, all of the lots in the auction were sold without reserves—meaning every toy had to be sold, however low the bid.

The auctioneer called out: "Lot 15, The Charles by George Brown, who would like to start the bidding on this lot at one dollar?" This loosened the room up and before long the bidding sailed over $100,000 and quickly ended at $231,000—setting a record for a toy at auction. The electricity in the auction gallery was fantastic. Overall, the entire auction of 361 lots of rare and desirable toys realized more than one million dollars.

Opposite page, top: The narrow bow and characteristic stenciling on this clockwork wind-up paddleboat are typical of the fine work on George Brown toys. Bottom: The Doctor's Buggy clearly illustrates the standard horse design used by the company. This page: Good examples showcasing George Brown's trademark design include, from top: a rare horse-drawn cigar wagon; a clockwork velocipede with a typical George Brown wind-up mechanism; Grand Central Depot tinplate horse drawn trolley; and a tinplate clockwork paddleboat shown with its original box.

Bru Jeune et CIE
Paris, France
1866 - 1899

Identification Clues

- Bisque heads on bisque shoulder plates with numbers and/or letters indicating size ranging from A – O incised on the back of the head and along the shoulder plate. A "circle dot" or "crescent" mark may also be incised along with "Bru Jne" on the backside of the head.

- Socket bisque head incised with the mark BRU Jne R

- Dolls with closed mouths or open/closed mouths are more valuable than those with open mouths

- Oval or square label on body indicating it is a Bru

BRU Jne R

The dolls produced by this company represent the so-called Golden Age of doll manufacturing, and the French dolls in particular are known for their beauty and artistry. Leon Casimir Bru founded his company in 1866 and produced dolls through the turn of the century. The porcelain-headed dolls with so-called "paperweight" glass eyes often have kid leather bodies with bisque arms or jointed wooden arms or all-wood bodies. Because Bru produced fewer pieces, with more intricate detail, than other competitors manufacturing dolls at the same time, Bru dolls are highly desirable today and command very high prices. Even in their day, the dolls Bru produced were quite expensive and were a wealthy child's plaything.

In 1883, the company was sold to Henry Celestin Chevrot, who continued the tradition of making dolls of high quality. Many consider this period the high point of Bru production. But by 1889, the company began to simplify the head designs and the overall quality of the dolls began to diminish. During this year a friend of Chevrot's, Paul Eugene Girard, took over the factory. Competition from the German doll manufacturers soon forced Girard to dramatically lower artistic standards in order to mass-produce pieces more simply. The dolls with open mouths, marked "Bru Jne R," were produced during this period. The company held together for ten more years until it became part of the Société Française de Fabrication de Bébés et Jouets (S.F.B.J.) in 1899.

Above: The Bru company made both beautiful porcelain children, left, and fashionable porcelain ladies, with beautifully sculpted faces and clothing of luxurious fabrics.

Buddy L
Moline, Illinois
1910 - 1939

Founded by Fred A. Lundahl, the Moline Pressed Steel Company began by producing steel fenders for International Harvester trucks. The company was based in Moline, Illinois, and the International Harvester contract provided the company with an abundance of work. Eventually the monotonous production of fenders took its toll on Lundahl, who wanted to make something special for his young son, Buddy. He gathered some scrap metal from the plant and fashioned a scale miniature version of a dining table and chairs. He continued to create such pieces for his son and in 1920,

when Buddy turned four, his father presented him with a reduced scale, open-bed pickup truck, which was an exact scaled-down version of the International Harvester trucks for which he manufactured fenders.

Young Buddy was thrilled with the toy, but it was the reaction from the neighborhood children that sparked Lundahl's creative mind to produce other trucks and to consider the possibilities of merchandising his creations. The quality, craftsmanship and attention to detail helped propel him into the toy-making spotlight. Starting with a limited line, he produced samples of trucks and a steam

Identification Clues

- Trucks marked with company logo "Buddy L Express Line"
- Usually marked on the sides of the vehicle
- Sturdy, well built with attention to detail
- Oversized vehicles in the early production were more than 20 inches in length

Above: Buddy L was known for its pressed-steel passenger vehicles, such as the railway express truck, top, which is 25 inches long, as well as industrial vehicles such as the U.S. Mail truck, above.

Top: These pressed-steel 28-inch-long passenger busses both have twenty-two chair seats and two benches. **Above:** An advertisement from *Child Life* magazine in December 1927 featured the story of Buddy L, along with examples of the company's products.

shovel as demonstration pieces during his presentations to F.A.O. Schwarz in New York and Marshall Field & Co. in Chicago. Both stores reacted positively to his line by placing huge orders for a fall delivery.

The first Buddy L toys made their debut in September 1921, just in time for the Christmas season. The company continued to produce truck parts, but expanded to include a toy division. By the end of 1923, only two years after its debut, the toy division led the company in sales. With the success of the Buddy L toys, the company changed its focus to become a toy producer exclusively. The line grew to include steamrollers, cranes and cement mixers. By 1926, sales offices were established throughout the country. The Buddy L cars and trucks were enjoying increased popularity and the demand for new items soared. The company decided to answer the consumer demand and

that year released a staggering twenty-nine different car and truck designs.

The company welcomed the 1930s with an official name change from the Moline Pressed Steel Company to Buddy L Manufacturing Company. Lundahl's nickname for his young son, Buddy Lundahl, became immortalized as a permanent namesake for one of American's favorite pressed steel toys. Until this time, the basic design element had been based on the International Harvester mold. With the advances in technology and industry this decade witnessed came changes such as pressed steel wheels and the use of real rubber tires. The most dramatic change took place around 1935, with the addition of electric headlamps to the cars and a total redesign of the entire truck line. It was at this time that large and strong toys for a child to ride began to be made. The line included removable saddle seats on some of the

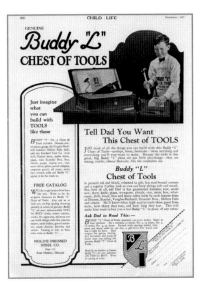

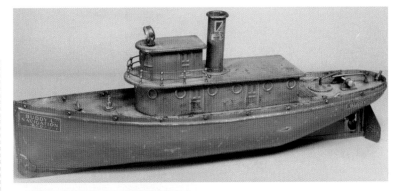

trucks, and featured advertisements from the period. An ad for Wrigley Chewing Gum on the sides of the trailer of the Railway Express truck was quite popular.

After the death of Fred A. Lundahl, the company was sold to J.W. Bettendorf. But the long-lasting effects of the Depression and the struggle to maintain a streamlined operation added up to failure to keep the company profitable. Buddy L was dissolved by a court order in 1939.

Top: Buddy L made a small line of industrial vehicles of wood to complement the pressed-steel pieces, such as these sleek trucks. **Above left:** An advertisement from *Child Life* in November 1927 featured the Buddy L chest of tools set. **Above:** In a rare departure from pressed-steel vehicles, Buddy L created a pressed-steel version of a classroom called the Laura Mae Play School. In order to stay competitive in the boat market, the company also manufactured a small number of ships. This dump truck was manufactured by Moline Pressed Steel, a descendant of Buddy L, after World War II.

Top: This pair of concrete mixers features mixing drums, base hoppers and cast wheels. **Above and right:** Buddy L's vast fleet of pressed-steel work trucks all measure more than 20 inches in length, and were capable of withstanding vigorous play.

Top: In the top row is a pair of pressed-steel Flivver trucks; the center row holds a Buddy L one-ton express truck and a Flivver "Huckster" Delivery truck; in the bottom row is a Flivver pick-up truck, a Flivver dump truck and a pressed steel Flivver coupe. **Left:** This pair of pressed-steel Buddy L stake trucks have black flat beds, disc wheels and aluminum tires. Note the variations in the back truck panels: one is open and the other is closed. Each truck is 25 inches long. **Above:** The pressed-steel Buddy L Robotoy is an electric toy that not only moves forward and back, but also dumps its cargo. It is controlled by a transformer.

Georges Carette et CIE
Nuremberg, Germany
1886 - 1917

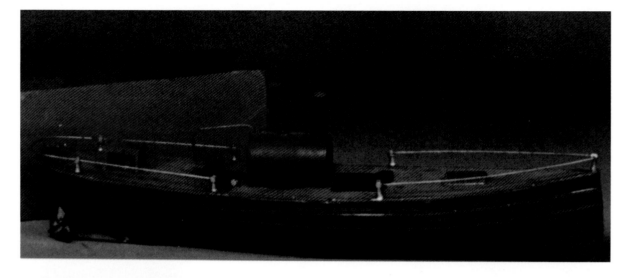

This German company with a reputation for quality and innovative toy designs was formed in 1886 by the Parisian Georges Carette as Georges Carette & CIE in Nuremberg, Germany. A family friend invested as a silent partner in the company, with major financial backing coming from a competitive German manufacturer, Gebruder Bing.

In 1893, at Chicago's Columbian Exposition, the company presented one of the earliest electric toy streetcars. Carette went on to dominate the field with production of both live-steam and spring-driven trains. Carette continued perfecting the process of lithography on metal and expanded production to include boats, cars and even magic lanterns.

The rumblings of World War I brought the production of toys nearly to a halt. Once the realities of the conflict became apparent, the French-born Carette, who was married to a German woman, was forced to leave Germany and his company behind. The company closed its doors for good in 1917.

Identification Clues

- Examine the piece for the logo, which is usually easy to find on the toy

- The toys have good details such as working lights on automobiles

- The toys have sturdy mechanisms and overall realism in their designs

Collector Alert
Look out for repainting or artificially distressed work on trains, boats and automobiles, which lowers the piece's value. Some pieces have chipped or missing paint, which is okay, provided other paint was not applied to the piece in an attempt to fix it up. The figures in the automobiles have often been repainted, repaired or even replaced.

Opposite page, top: This is a fine example of a streamlined, steam-powered tinplate boat manufactured by Carette. **Center, bottom, and this page:** These open touring cars and limousines illustrate the quality of design and diversity of production that established Carette as a popular manufacturer of automobiles.

Chad Valley
Birmingham, England
1897 - 1978

Identification Clues

- Embroidered label reads: "HYGIENIC TOYS MADE IN ENGLAND BY CHAD VALLEY CO. LTD
- Toys made after 1938 are marked with the Royal Crest and the above wording
- Bears made from 1920 – 1930 are tagged in the ears with buttons of metal and a celluloid center marked "Chad Valley Aerolite Trade Mark." Aerolite refers to the kapok stuffing used in the bears.
- After 1930 bears, animals and dolls all had a label with the above wording on the foot
- Chad Valley bears are distinguished by their thick oval noses

The Johnson brothers, Joseph and Alfred, first formed a printing business called Johnson Bros. Ltd. in 1820. In 1897 the company relocated to Harborne on the river Chad, and the name was changed to reflect their new location. As Chad Valley, the company began producing games, puzzles, toys and bears and felt dolls. In 1920, the company moved again, taking over the Wrekin Toy Works in Shropshire but retaining the Chad Valley name, which, by then, was well known as a maker of toys of high quality. The Chad Valley teddy bear was offered in thirteen different sizes with six different qualities of material. Among their best-known dolls were the 1938 portraits of Princess Elizabeth and Princess Margaret Rose in matching pink and blue felt coats and hats.

The quality of the toys was so good that in 1938 the company was granted a Royal Warrant of Appointment as Toymakers to Her Majesty the Queen.

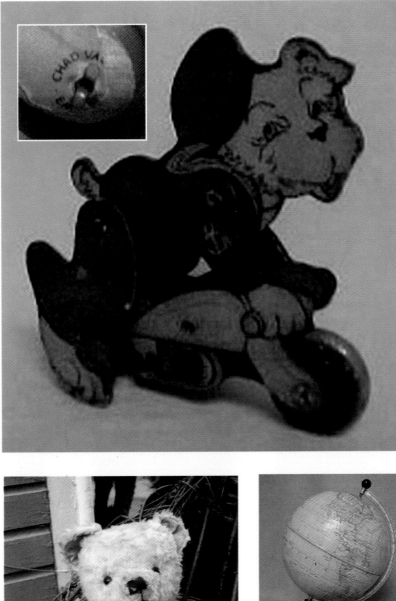

Opposite page, top: Chad Valley began making its teddy bears in 1915-1916. The 27-inch bear at right is circa 1930 and has an identification tag on its foot and a celluloid button in the right ear. Bottom: The Chad Valley logo is prominently displayed on this lithographed tinplate wind-up race car. This page, top left: This whimsical toy is die-cut paper on wood. Far left: Another circa-1930s teddy bear, this white alpaca example is about 30 inches high. It has beige kid leather on the inside of its ears, and an embroidered nose and mouth. Above left and left: Chad Valley made a diverse range of toys, including this tinplate lithographed globe and colorful lithographed sand toys.

Character Toy and Novelty Company
South Norwalk, Connecticut
Late 1920s - 1983

The bears manufactured by this American toy company turn up all over the country today. Character began manufacturing bears in the 1920s. These had cloth tags that read: "Character, Designed by Character Novelty Co Inc., So Norwalk Conn." Some of the bears made during the 1930s were not fully jointed, and had metal noses similar to those on the bears produced by the Knickerbocker Company. Character also entered into a licensing agreement with the Walt Disney company to manufacture plush character items for them.

The success of Character can be credited to two New Yorkers, Caesar Mangiapani and Jack Levy, who joined the company after World War II. Mangiapani expanded the line of toys to include a wider variety of animals, including teddy bears. He was responsible for the designs that captured the imaginations of children everywhere. Levy managed the sales end of the business, putting the Character products into every major department store across the country.

When the pair joined the company, the United States was going through a post-war boom, with more babies being born than during any other period in history and the bears and toys of the Character Toy and Novelty Company were in great demand. Levy retired in 1960, but the company continued making playthings for twenty more years with Caesar Mangiapani at the design helm until his death in 1983.

Above: Character Toy and Novelty manufactured these crude plush representations of the Disney characters Pluto, left, and Bambi, right, in the 1930s and 1940s.

Collector Alert

This company's bears are often confused with the Knickerbocker bears from the same time period. They have lots of personality and were mass-produced using cheap materials. The value is slowly rising on the early mohair bears, if they are in very good condition.

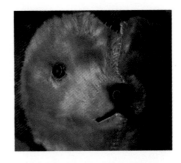

Above left: The felt behind the eyes adds personality to this teddy bear, and is a characteristic of the bears and animals made by the Character Toy and Novelty Company. **Left:** The company also interpreted Disney's Donald Duck. **Above:** This bear design features a metal nose with contrasting facial color.

Martha Jenks Chase
Rhode Island
1889 - 1930 (possibly later)

Identification Clues

- Some dolls were tagged with a paper label "The Chase Stockinet Doll, Made of Stockinet and cloth, Stuffed with cotton, Painted by hand, Made by Especially Trained workers."

PAWTUCKET R.I.
MADE IN U.S.A.

Above: This 24-inch doll by Martha Chase has a stockinet head stretched over a mask, features hand painted in oil and molded, painted hair.

In the late 1880s this American dollmaker began producing dolls with heads of stockinet (an elastic fabric knitted from silk or cotton) stretched over a mask, hand oil-painted features and molded, painted hair. She made them first to give away, but eventually they came to the attention of stores, and demand for them grew. As they gained popularity, Chase was asked to make a large, waterproof size to use in hospital training schools. By 1917, they were also used in child welfare work. The hospital dolls are very heavy, as they were weighted to be as heavy as a child of equivalent size.

The early Chase dolls have sateen torsos, while the later ones often have rough stockinet bodies with a water-proof finish. They were stitch-jointed at the shoulders, hips and knees. Later dolls were jointed only at the hips and shoulders. Some had applied thumbs. All the dolls carried the company mark on the thigh or under the arm, but often this has been rubbed off. Applied ears and painted features and hair are all trademarks of the Chase dolls, which included babies, children and even an Alice in Wonderland character doll.

After Martha Chase died in 1925, her family continued to make the dolls. It is not clear exactly when they ceased production, but it has been reported that a grandson, Robert Chase, was making vinyl-headed dolls into the 1970s.

J. Chein & Company
Harrison, New Jersey
1903 - 1979

The company was founded in 1903 by Julius Chein and was located in New York City. The company specialized in lithographed tin mechanical toys, and developed a special production process of printing the design and color first on the sheet of tin, then pressing it into shape. This process allowed the company to mass-produce huge quantities of toys very inexpensively. To accommodate an expanding production line, the company relocated in 1912 to Harrison, New Jersey.

America's response to the aggression in Germany prior to World War I was an embargo on all German products shipped to the United States. As a result of the embargo, the Chein Company increased their toy production and cornered the American market of tin lithographed mechanical playthings. From this period through the 1950s, Chein mass-produced mechanical toys and focused its line on ferris wheels; roller coasters; rocket ride toys; tin banks; automobiles and trucks. In 1926, in the midst of the company's expansion, Julius Chein met his untimely death during a horseback ride in Central Park. Faced with the increasing popularity of their toy line, his wife, Elizabeth Chein, took the helm of the company, with the assistance of her brother, Samuel Hoffman. Together they managed to successfully continue Julius's legacy.

Identification Clues

- Toys are marked with company name
- Toys are colorful and lightweight
- Toys in the box are more desirable and often priced higher
- Lots of examples are still available in the marketplace

Above: Chein & Company's figural lithographed tinplate banks were colorful and whimsical. **Left:** Among Chein & Company's offerings were simplistic lithographed wind-up trucks, like this example.

Above right: Circus figures, like this colorful clown, were popular subjects for Chein's lithographed tinplate banks. **Right:** A monkey perpetually tips his hat in gratitude on this lithographed tinplate still bank.

Top: Chein's depiction of one of the Three Little Pigs' homes graces this lithographed tinplate still bank. Left: A colorful lithographed tin clown puncher with a celluloid punching bag is supported on a spring stand with a clockwork mechanism. Above: This lithographed tin and celluloid wind-up Popeye puncher dates from the 1930s.

Top: This example of Chein & Company's lithographed tin roller coaster still has its original box. The wind-up toy has curved tracks. **Above:** These Popeye and Barnacle Bill lithographed tin wind-up toys have clockwork mechanisms. **Right:** The same characters of Popeye and Barnacle Bill were also made as wind-up toys wearing barrels.

Above: Chein & Company's ferris wheel, shown with its original box, is lithographed tin with clockwork activation. **Left**: Boxers Popeye and Barnacle Bill are lithographed tinplate clockwork wind-up toys with celluloid punching bags.

Chiltern
Buckinghamshire, England
1921 - 1964

Identification Clues

- Tag sewn into side seam of bear "Chiltern Hygienic Toys Made in England"
- Glass eyes
- May also wear paper tags that read "Chiltern Hygienic Toys Made in England" or "Made in England, Chiltern Toys, Awarded the Certificate of the Institute of Hygiene"
- Velvet or velveteen paw pads

Leon Rees inherited the Chiltern Toy Works in 1919, upon the death of his father-in-law and business partner, Josef Eisenmann. In 1920 Rees joined forces with Harry Stone, who had been working at J.K. Farnell, to manufacture soft toys and dolls in 1920. Officially H.G. Stone & Co. Ltd., the company was known as Chiltern because of its location in the Chiltern Hills in Bucking-hamshire. The name Chiltern Toys first appeared in a trade magazine in 1923, the same year the first line of "Hugmee" bears was introduced. These became especially popular in the 1940s and 1950s, and are the most common Chiltern bears to show up at appraisal fairs. The Hugmee bears have glass eyes, are fully jointed with kapok or cotton stuffing, and are usually mohair. They usually have a cloth tag on the side seam printed: "Chiltern Hygienic Toys Made in England." The bears usually also had a squeaker and a chest tag reading "I Growl." Some versions include a Swiss music box in the torso of the bear.

In 1940 the factory had to stop making toys to focus on war work, although some toys continued to be made throughout the war at the company's other factories. The company was taken over by Dunbee-Combex-Marx in 1964 and then by Chad Valley in 1967.

Above: One of Chiltern's most popular bears was the Hugmee model, circa 1940. This golden mohair example is 14 inches high and has kapok stuffing and amber glass eyes.

Charles M. Crandall
Covington, Pennsylvania
1820 - 1905

C harles M. Crandall worked with his father, Asa Crandall, who had founded the family woodworking factory in 1820 in Covington, Pennsylvania. When Charles was sixteen years old his father died, and the family's woodworking business passed into his young hands. It was 1867, post Civil War, and the United States economy was booming. Over the next decade, the factory produced a variety of furniture pieces and wooden items, including a successful and popular wooden croquet game set packaged in a wooden box. The boxes for the set were produced with tongue-and-groove corners, which would eventually shape and change the direction of the company. Occasionally Crandall brought home the grooved scraps from the croquet set boxes for his children. They never seemed to exhaust the infinite possibilities of the grooved corners and found constant delight in the wooden scraps. Watching the children's playful delight inspired Crandall to create his first children's play set: "Crandall Building Blocks," a set of interlocking grooved wooden toys that nearly sold out its entire production in the first year. He patented this concept in 1867.

It was Crandall's imagination and ingenuity with the interlocking design that gave his toys appeal and popularity. His most recognized and greatest product that made use of this concept was "The Acrobats." The interlocking concept was also applied to Crandall's District School 1875; Crandall's Wide-Awake Alphabet; Crandall's Heavy Artillery soldier blocks and the Crandall Menagerie.

As the business continued to grow and prosper, Crandall moved the expanding operation to Montrose, Pennsylvania, in 1875. By 1885 he had moved to Waverly, New York and established the Waverly Toy Works. The business in Montrose was handed over to Crandall's son, Fredrick, but one year later, in 1886, a fire devastated the factory and the remainder of the operation was moved to Elkland, Pennsylvania. Production resumed through the turn of the century, but the factory finally closed its doors in 1907. Charles Crandall died in 1905.

Crandall's toys continue to amaze and delight collectors today. The quality and simplicity capture the time period brilliantly. All of the Crandall toys were packaged in wood boxes as opposed to paper boxes, which explains why pieces found today have survived the elements and effects of aging, and are usually intact and in good condition.

Identification Clues

- Look for the label on the box
- Interlocking wooden hinges
- Come in play sets and groups of items

Top right: The Acrobats set, top right, was the most recognized toy to exemplify Crandall's concept of interlocking grooved wooden pieces. Other popular toys were his Treasure Blocks and Heavy Artillery sets, shown on a catalog page, **above right**.

Jesse Crandall

Brooklyn, New York
1840s - 1880s

Identification Clues

- Toys are unmarked, so positive identification is difficult

- Check for patent numbers from the 1860s -1880s (*see Reference section*)

- Simplistic lines and folk-art look coupled with lack of any other company's identifiying marks

Above: While it is difficult to firmly identify pieces by Jesse Crandall, this early American rocking horse, circa 1860s, is attributed to the prolific maker by its simplistic lines and folk-art aesthetic.

Jesse Crandall, who was born in 1833, often recalled that some of his earliest memories from childhood were of being taught to carve wooden animals at the age of five. His father, Benjamin P. Crandall, set up a toy manufacturing business in New York City around 1840. Jesse Crandall worked with his father and by 1859 had patented his first toy, a rocking horse. After the Civil War, Jesse moved to Brooklyn and started his own business. He produced toys like the shoofly rocker and two spring-activated hobbyhorses. He also was responsible for the production of velocipedes; carriages; stick horses; construction toys; blocks; and an elevated wooden railroad.

Shortly after celebrating his eightieth birthday, Crandall was quoted in a 1913 interview as saying, "My first patent was taken out in 1859 for a spring horse. The Prince of Wales rode one and you see what a horse-man he has developed into now!" While a variety of inventors give credit to teachers or individuals who may have inspired their work, Crandall credited his vivid dreams while he slept for the inspiration of his new toy creations. "The alarm of the future rings me up, and I am on the carpet in a second with my pad on my knee," was the creed he lived by. In addition to the spring horse patent, he is recognized as the creator of the velocipede in 1868. The genius and simplicity of Crandall's patented designs were admired by the buying public and copied by other manufacturers, which prompted this response, "You get a piece of paper but you do not get protection till you have spent a lot of money in court to keep up the dignity of that same patent." This particular member of the very talented Crandall family most likely continued carving toys right up to the day he died.

Daisy Manufacturing Company, Inc.
Plymouth, Michigan
1888

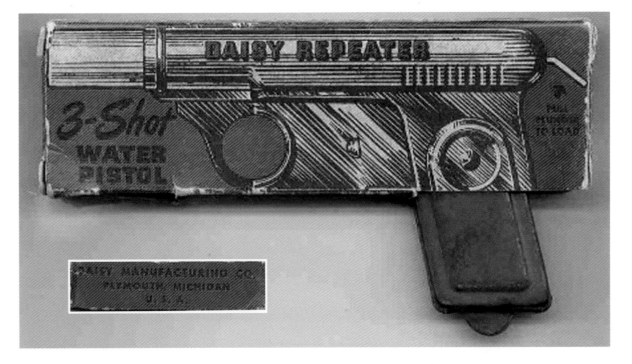

This company's success is a fine example of necessity being the mother of invention. The corporate roots can be traced back to the early 1880s in Plymouth, Michigan, when the Plymouth Iron Windmill Company began manufacturing iron windmills for use on farms throughout the Midwest and Great Plains regions. As sales began dying down, the company decided to develop an innovative product to attract new customers. In 1886 Plymouth company inventor Clarence Hamilton introduced his revolutionary invention during a company board meeting. His novelty item was a combination of metal and wire, vaguely resembling a gun that could fire a lead ball using compressed air. During his demonstration, then-president of the company Lewis Cass Hough gave the gun a try and after his first shot enthusiastically exclaimed, "Boy that's a daisy!" The name stuck, and the very first BB gun went into production as a premium (gift with purchase) item given to farmers when they purchased a windmill. The BB gun took off like a shot, and in its first year of production the company manufactured eighty-six thousand guns. Production doubled the following year. Before long the company was manufacturing more Daisy BB guns then windmills, so on January 26, 1895, the company's board of directors officially voted to change the name to Daisy Manufacturing Company, Inc.

The air rifles continued to be popular for many years. As the country entered into the late 1920s, the funny papers and its comic-strip characters were becoming a significant part of American popular culture. The early comic-strip characters from the first funny papers are credited with helping Americans keep their minds off the anxieties of the Great Depression, as well as with keeping many toy companies in business. Daisy was one of these companies. The firm first latched onto a futuristic comic hero named Buck Rogers whose adventures as a spaceman in the twenty-fifth-century proved popular with American adults and children alike. The strip, which began in 1929, generated toys and premiums from several companies, but it was Daisy that capitalized on the strip's popularity by creating several versions of Buck

Identification Clues

- Early guns are marked "DAISY MFD. BY IRON WIND MILL CO. PLYMOUTH MICH. PAT. APD. FOR"

- Later guns are marked DAISY MFG along with a name or a single letter or a combination of letters and numbers or a number and model number. i.e. No. 121 Model 40

- Names of some of the Daisy guns include "Bulls Eye, Dewey, Hero, Dandy, and Atlas"

- All Daisy products have the name of the company and patent information somewhere on the item

Above: This metal three-shot water pistol Daisy Repeater still has its original colorful cardboard packaging.

Daisy Manufacturing Company, Inc.

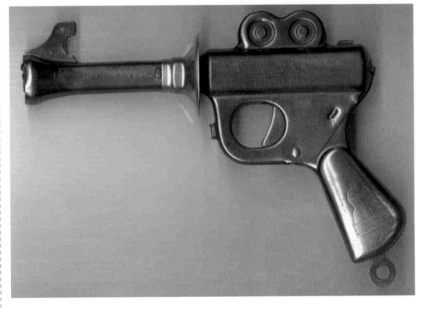

Rogers' Atomic Detonator Pistol. This toy continued to keep the company's ledger in the black.

Next the company turned to a cowboy who first appeared in the comic pages in 1935 as Bronc Peeler. By 1938, the character evolved into Red Ryder. Even though Red was a secondary character in the comic strip, in 1939 he became better known as the cowpoke with a rifle named after him. The company's most popular cre-

ation, the Daisy Red Ryder, coveted by every young American boy, turned the company into a household name. More than nine million Red Ryders were sold.

The company has maintained continuous production since that time. Based in Rogers, Arkansas, since 1958, today Daisy is considered the world's oldest and largest manufacturer of air guns, ammo and accessories.

Top: Daisy's Pop Pistol was manufactured in lithographed tinplate. **Above:** The Pop Pistol's handle featured the company's slogan: "It's a Daisy." **Above right:** Daisy made the metal Buck Roger's Atomic Detonator Pistol in the 1930s.

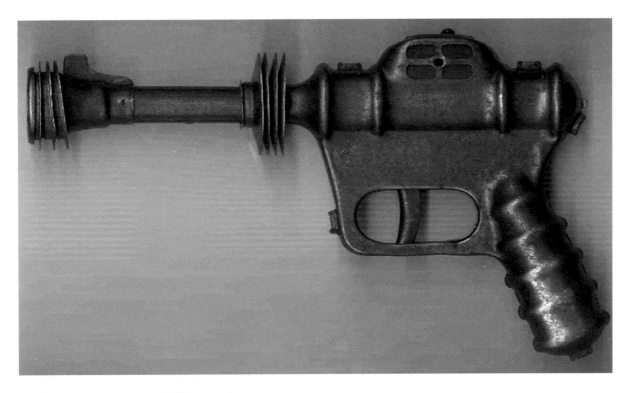

Top: The popular Buck Roger's Atomic Detonator Pistol was manufactured in several versions; note the difference in design between this one and the one on the facing page. **Above left:** The logo on Buck Roger's Atomic Detonator Pistol featured the popular comic-strip character. **Left:** This metal water pistol worked when the front of it was placed in water and the metal lever was pulled back.

Dean's Rag Book Co. Ltd.
London and South Wales, England
1903

Identification Clues

- Early tags on the foot of the dolls feature their logo of two dogs fighting over a rag book and the words: MADE IN GREAT BRITIAN BY DEAN'S RAG BOOK CO. LTD.

- Later tags say: DEAN'S HYGENIC TOYS, MADE IN ENGLAND BY DEAN'S RAG BOOK CO. LTD.

Above: This Mickey Mouse Jazzer still has its original box and instruction sheet. Mickey has button eyes, a toothy grin and five fingered hands. His long tail was designed to be clipped to a gramophone, which allowed Mickey to dance an amazing variety of jazz steps.

This company has its roots in a family business that dates back to the eighteenth century. Henry Samuel Dean founded the Dean's Rag Book Co. Ltd. in 1903 as a subsidiary of the Dean and Son printing and publishing company that had been in existence for more than one hundred years already. Rag books were first designed for babies. They featured illustrated toys and animals, and were made to be washable. The company continued to produce dolls and characters from children's books, and in 1910 registered their logo of two dogs fighting over a cloth book.

Dean's first made its own teddy bears in 1915, though it is believed that they may have been making bears for other companies before this time. During the 1920s the firm manufactured pull toys, soft animals, golliwoggs and teddy bears. Golliwoggs were the collaborative brainchild of Florence K. Upton and her sister Bertha. Florence created the drawings for children's books while Bertha wrote of the adventures of the golli. Some say this black-skinned character with bushy hair and large red lips was inspired by the dark-skinned natives who worked with the British soldiers in occupied Egypt around 1895, but Florence Upton's memoirs claim that the character was inspired by a toy she found in the attic of her childhood home. The children's stories were very popular in Great Britain, and the golliwog also became well-known as a promotional figure for a variety of products.

Dean's manufactured the first Mickey Mouse for Walt Disney in the 1930s and continues to manufacture mohair teddy bears of high quality, that are fully jointed, stuffed with kapok and have glass eyes.

Dent Hardware Company
Fullerton, Pennsylvania
1895 - 1937

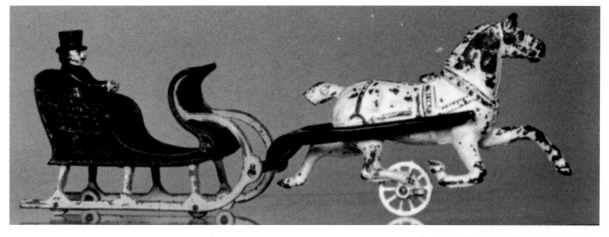

One version of the American dream was realized by English immigrant Henry H. Dent, who joined forces with four partners in 1895 to produce cast-iron hardware for refrigerators and cold storage units, in addition to cast-iron toys. The company soon gained a reputation for exceptional casting.

The attention to detail and the quality of their casting techniques provided the company with the distinction of producing the finest automotive toys of the 1920s. American toy manufacturers had perfected the skill of using cast iron that was not duplicated by any other foreign toy manufacturer. Dent also experimented with other materials like cast aluminum, but found it a difficult material to manipulate. So cast iron became the material of choice for the company, which produced a variety of toys in this material. All forms of transportation were subjects of their toy design: boats; trains; airplanes; fire wagons; horse-drawn carriages; and mechanical banks.

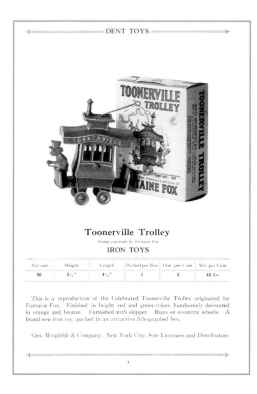

⊰======= DENT TOYS =======⊱

Toonerville Trolley
Design copyright by Fontaine Fox
IRON TOYS

Number	Height	Length	Packed per Box	Doz. per Case	Wt. per Case
50	5⅛"	4⅝"	1	3	43 lbs.

This is a reproduction of the Celebrated Toonerville Trolley originated by Fontaine Fox. Finished in bright red and green colors, handsomely decorated in orange and bronze. Furnished with skipper. Runs on eccentric wheels. A brand new iron toy, packed in an attractive lithographed box.

Geo. Borgfeldt & Company, New York City, Sole Licensees and Distributors.

5

Above: This cast-iron horse-drawn sleigh, circa 1910, has paint loss and wear throughout that is typical of toys this age. **Left:** This page highlighting Dent Toys from a George Borgfeldt catalog features the popular Toonerville Trolley.

Dirigibles

Number 656 Dirigible finished in bright aluminum paint, with red and blue trimmings, mounted on nickel-plated disc wheels, red centers.

Number 661 Dirigible, in bright colors, with trimmings, mounted on nickel-plated red centered disc wheels.

Numbers 655, 654 and 644 Dirigibles, finished in assorted colors in a box striped with colors and mounted on nickel-plated disc wheels.

IRON TOYS

Number	Name	Length	Height	Packed per Box	Dozen per Case	Weight per Case
656	Los Angeles	12⅝″	4⅜″	1	1	36 lbs.
661	Los Angeles	10¾″	3⅞″	1	1	32 lbs.
655	Los Angeles	8¾″	3¼″	3	3	47 lbs.
654	Zep	6¾″	2¾″	6	6	106 lbs.
644	Zep	5″	1½″	12	12	50 lbs.

Number 3655 Los Angeles, same size as number 655, polished aluminum; packed 3 in a box; 3 dozen per case; weight per case, 22 lbs.

Number 2654 Zep, same size as number 654, polished aluminum; packed 6 in a box; 6 dozen per case; weight per case, 25 lbs.

Number 1644 Zep, same size as number 644, polished aluminum; packed 12 in a box; 12 dozen per case; weight per case, 23 lbs.

Made of cast aluminum, highly polished, trimmed in red. Disc wheels. Exceedingly light in weight, most attractive in appearance.

14

Above: This cast aluminum Los Angeles Dirigible is circa 1920s. **Right:** The variations available are featured on this catalog page, along with other Dent offerings of that decade.

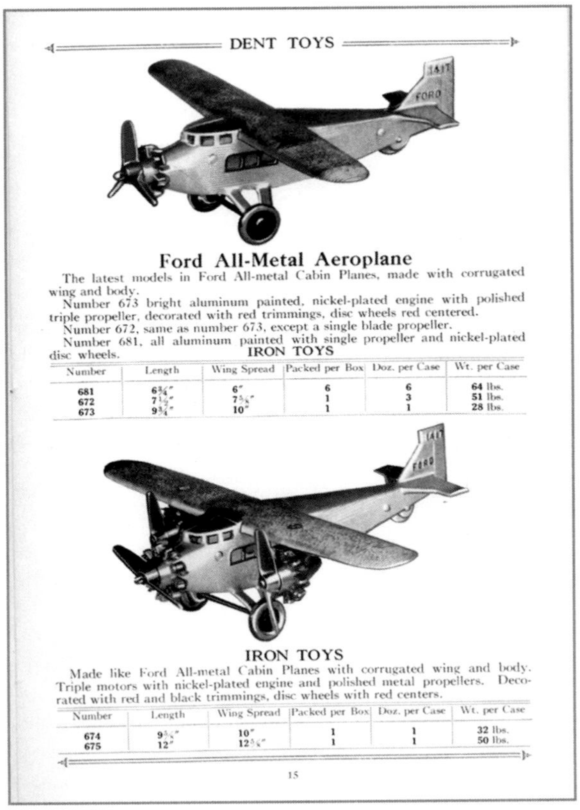

DENT TOYS

Ford All-Metal Aeroplane

The latest models in Ford All-metal Cabin Planes, made with corrugated wing and body.

Number 673 bright aluminum painted, nickel-plated engine with polished triple propeller, decorated with red trimmings, disc wheels red centered.

Number 672, same as number 673, except a single blade propeller.

Number 681, all aluminum painted with single propeller and nickel-plated disc wheels.

IRON TOYS

Number	Length	Wing Spread	Packed per Box	Doz. per Case	Wt. per Case
681	6¾"	6"	6	6	64 lbs.
672	7½"	7⅝"	1	3	51 lbs.
673	9¾"	10"	1	1	28 lbs.

IRON TOYS

Made like Ford All-metal Cabin Planes with corrugated wing and body. Triple motors with nickel-plated engine and polished metal propellers. Decorated with red and black trimmings, disc wheels with red centers.

Number	Length	Wing Spread	Packed per Box	Doz. per Case	Wt. per Case
674	9⅝"	10"	1	1	32 lbs.
675	12"	12⅝"	1	1	50 lbs.

15

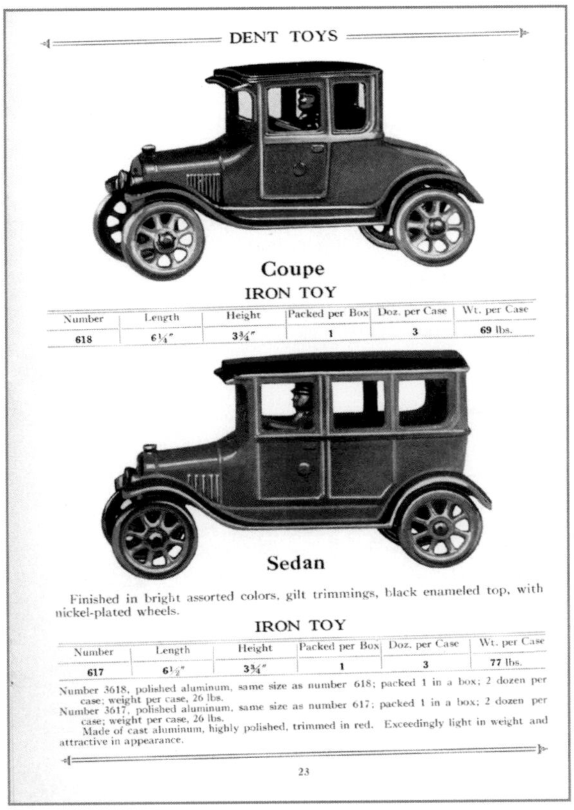

DENT TOYS

Coupe

IRON TOY

Number	Length	Height	Packed per Box	Doz. per Case	Wt. per Case
618	6¼"	3¾"	1	3	69 lbs.

Sedan

Finished in bright assorted colors, gilt trimmings, black enameled top, with nickel-plated wheels.

IRON TOY

Number	Length	Height	Packed per Box	Doz. per Case	Wt. per Case
617	6½"	3¾"	1	3	77 lbs.

Number 3618, polished aluminum, same size as number 618; packed 1 in a box; 2 dozen per case; weight per case, 26 lbs.

Number 3617, polished aluminum, same size as number 617; packed 1 in a box; 2 dozen per case; weight per case, 26 lbs.

Made of cast aluminum, highly polished, trimmed in red. Exceedingly light in weight and attractive in appearance.

23

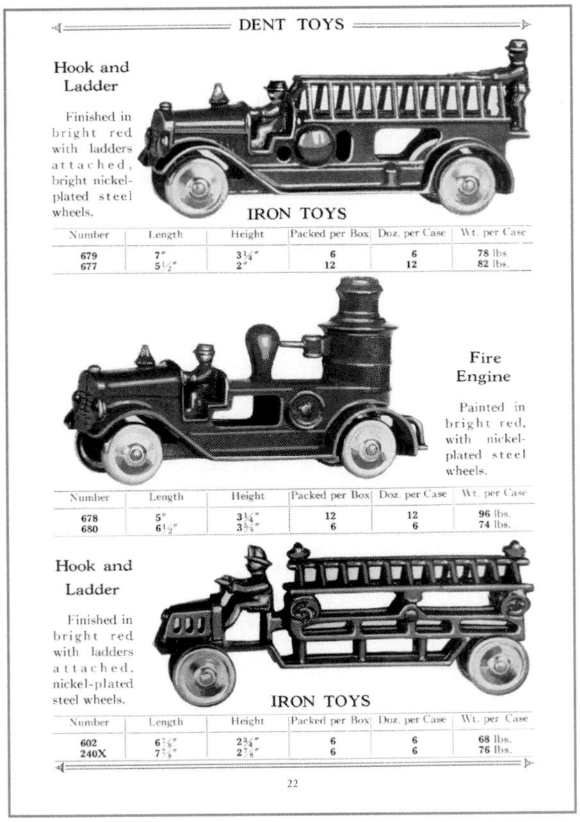

DENT TOYS

Hook and Ladder

Finished in bright red with ladders attached, bright nickel-plated steel wheels.

IRON TOYS

Number	Length	Height	Packed per Box	Doz. per Case	Wt. per Case
679	7"	3¼"	6	6	78 lbs.
677	5½"	2"	12	12	82 lbs.

Fire Engine

Painted in bright red, with nickel-plated steel wheels.

Number	Length	Height	Packed per Box	Doz. per Case	Wt. per Case
678	5"	3¼"	12	12	96 lbs.
680	6½"	3⅝"	6	6	74 lbs.

Hook and Ladder

Finished in bright red with ladders attached, nickel-plated steel wheels.

IRON TOYS

Number	Length	Height	Packed per Box	Doz. per Case	Wt. per Case
602	6⅞"	2¾"	6	6	68 lbs.
240X	7⅞"	2⅞"	6	6	76 lbs.

22

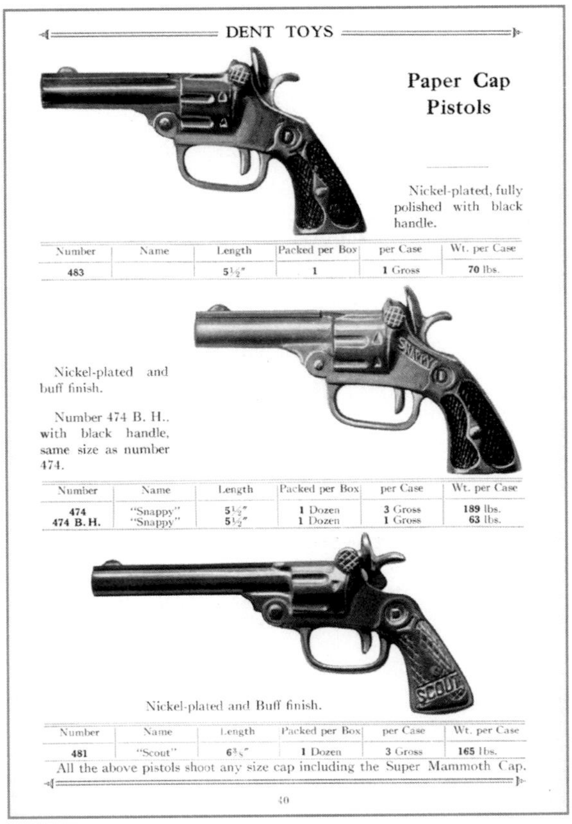

DENT TOYS

Paper Cap Pistols

Nickel-plated, fully polished with black handle.

Number	Name	Length	Packed per Box	per Case	Wt. per Case
483		5½"	1	1 Gross	70 lbs.

Nickel-plated and buff finish.

Number 474 B. H., with black handle, same size as number 474.

Number	Name	Length	Packed per Box	per Case	Wt. per Case
474	"Snappy"	5½"	1 Dozen	3 Gross	189 lbs.
474 B. H.	"Snappy"	5½"	1 Dozen	1 Gross	63 lbs.

Nickel-plated and Buff finish.

Number	Name	Length	Packed per Box	per Case	Wt. per Case
481	"Scout"	6⅜"	1 Dozen	3 Gross	165 lbs.

All the above pistols shoot any size cap including the Super Mammoth Cap.

40

Above: These pages from a Dent Hardware Company catalog from the 1920s illustrate the diversity of products manufactured by the company during that era. While the firm experimented with various materials, the one of choice was usually cast iron, especially for its transportation toys. Dent is usually credited as being the maker of the finest automotive toys of the 1920s.

Duncan
Los Angeles, California
1928

Identification Clues

- Duncan made wooden, plastic, lithographed tinplate and butterfly yo-yos
- In the 1950s and 1960s Duncan manufactured advertising yo-yos for companies like 7-Up, Coca-Cola, Kitty Clover Potato Chips, Rice Krispies and Whirlpool
- All Duncan yo-yos are clearly marked "Duncan"

The yo-yo might possibly be the oldest toy that has been slightly modified over time but is still being produced and enjoyed today. The history of this toy dates back to stone yo-yos discovered in archeological digs from ancient Greece, and evidence indicates that the "to-and-fro" toy may have been present in ancient Chinese culture thousands of years ago. During the 1700s the yo-yo or—as it was called by the French–"jou-jou," entertained the royal court, while a century later the toy became popular with the children of Victorian England. By the end of the 1800s, patents and design changes were granted and filed in the United States. Ironically, by the early 1900s the toy lost its appeal for Americans, and the yo-yo would lie dormant for nearly thirty years.

It took the entrepreneur responsible for marketing the parking meter, movie screen and Eskimo pies to revitalize the popularity of the yo-yo, lifting it to pop-culture status. In 1928 Donald Duncan's path crossed with Pedro Flores, who was demonstrating how to play with a yo-yo in Los Angels, California. Duncan was immediately fascinated by the simple toy and offered $25,000 to buy Flores's small company called The Yo-Yo Manufacturing Company. A proven master marketer, Duncan hired a platoon of "yo-yo men" to travel the country demonstrating the amazing yo-yo tricks called "around the world" and "walking the dog." These traveling road shows generated great excitement across the country, along with tremendous sales for the company.

Needless to say, the popularity of the yo-yo lives on today and has transcended even Duncan's early fascination with the toy. Three American presidents, John F. Kennedy, Lyndon Johnson and Richard Nixon, have publicly played with the toy, and in 1992 a yo-yo was taken on board the space shuttle Atlantis by astronaut Jeffrey Hoffman.

Above: The popular Butterfly yo-yo by Duncan, circa 1940s, came complete with instructions for a variety of tournament tricks. **Left:** This Duncan plastic Glow Imperial yo-yo features the popular Rice Krispies cereal trio: Snap, Krackle and Pop.

Effanbee

New York, New York
1910

One of the most important American doll companies, which is still producing dolls today, this firm was started by Walter Fleischaker & Hugo Baum, two Atlantic City, New Jersey, shopkeepers, who initially sold toys and dolls in their adjoining shops. They began manufacturing dolls in 1913, when doll manufacturing in American was still quite young, and many companies looked to the European makers to create dolls. Effanbee (formed by the initials of its founders' last names, and sometimes seen written as EFFanBEE), began by specializing in composition baby dolls, but by 1915, the company was producing more than one hundred other varieties of dolls. Early characters included Aunt Dinah, Baby Bright Eyes, Baby Grumpy, Baby Huggins, Baby Snowball, Mary Jane and, in 1917, the War Nurse, which came in three sizes, ranging from 12 to 24 inches, and wore copies of official uniforms. The dolls were all marked on the back or under the hairline with the name of the company and sometimes with the name of the doll. The early pieces either had molded short hair or human-hair wigs. The bodies were either cloth or fully-jointed composition.

By 1919 Effanbee was making more than three hundred different dolls, including a Mama doll, which was one of the models with a label stating: "They Walk, They Talk, They Sleep." In 1926 the popular Bubbles, a composition shoulder-head baby with composition arms, molded hair and a cloth body, was introduced. The doll had dimples, and an open mouth with two teeth; and its left forefinger was designed to fit into its mouth. Other manufacturers tried to copy this design, and Effanbee was granted two injunctions against competitors' infringements.

Right after Bubbles, one of the most popular Effanbee designs was the Patsy doll, designed in 1927 by the prolific Bernard Lipfert, who designed dolls for most major

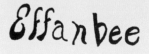
Above: This grouping of Effanbee composition dolls includes several variations of the popular Patsy. **From left,** the dolls are: Patsy-Joan; Patsy, with molded hair; Patsy-Ann, with molded hair; Patricia; Patsy-Ann, with molded hair; and Patsy with a brown mohair wig.

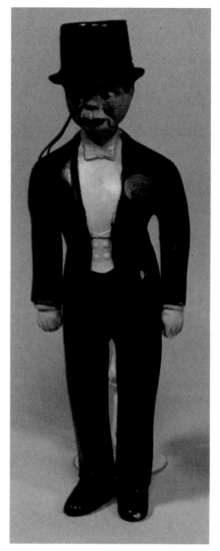

Collector Alert
Be sure there is little or no crazing in the eyes of the doll as this lowers its value. Be sure to store/display the doll out of direct sunlight and in a constant moderate temperature/humidity location. Extremes on either end will cause permanent damage.

American doll manufacturers in the first half of the twentieth century. Originally called Mimi, Patsy was made in a variety of sizes, including an "older sister," Patsy Ann, in 1929, and a tiny Patsykins in 1930, as well as black and white versions. The doll's design was a revolutionary one, having an all-composition body with a ball neck going into a socket head, one arm bent and straight legs. It was jointed at the neck, shoulders and

hips, and had short molded hair. Again, Effanbee had to go to court to stop imitations.

In 1936 Effanbee was named by *Fortune* magazine as one of the country's three major doll manufacturers, along with the Alexander Doll Company and the Ideal Toy and Novelty Company. It has had several owners since the original Fleischaker and Baum, and continues to be a major American doll company today.

Above left: This 25-inch composition Patsy Ruth features sleep eyes. **Above right:** In the late 1930s the company produced a rubber Charlie McCarthy, painted in the familiar black-and-white suit and wearing a button with his name on it.

Above left: This 14-inch composition Patsy, left, still has her original box; the 16-inch composition Patsy Joan has slimmer legs than many of the dolls in the Patsy family. Left: This 14-inch Skippy in uniform, left, and 14-inch Baby Grumpy are both marked composition dolls. Skippy is marked on the back of his head: Effanbee, Skippy, © P.L. Crosby. This character was first made in 1929 as a companion to Patsy. The Baby Grumpy character is one of the earliest, first produced in 1915. He is marked on the back of his shoulderplate; Effanbee Dolls, Walk. Talk. Sleep and also bears a marked tag on his shorts as well as the Effanbee heart button. Above: Marilee is a 30-inch composition shoulder-head doll with sleep eyes. This character was first produced in 1929. She is marked on the back of her shoulder plate: Effanbee, Marilee, Copyr.

James Fallows & Sons
Philadelphia, Pennsylvania
1874 - 1890s

Identification Clues

- "IXL" usually marked on the bottom of the toy
- Lightweight tinplate toys with stenciling
- Toys are simplistic in design

An early pioneer in the world of toy production, James Fallows, a young English designer and inventor, began his career by working with Francis, Field and Francis in Philadelphia, Pennsylvania, around 1870. Together they manufactured a variety of early tinplate toys that were a direct reflection of society during the later part of the nineteenth century, including toy versions of horse-drawn carriages and paddleboats. It was, however, the production of the more practical houseware items and utensils that paid the bills in the early stages of the company's development. In 1874 Fallows established his own tinware firm in Philadelphia.

By 1877, Fallows had fashioned and perfected his own process to emboss designs on tinplate, practically an art form in itself, and had the entire process patented. These highly decorative designs and Fallows` personal trademark, IXL, which stands for I excel, make identification of a Fallows-designed toy easy. With his newly patented embossing process, Fallows ventured into creating his own business of toy design and manufacturing. The toys he designed during this period are distinguished by a pleasing simplicity and artistry.

For most of the following two decades, Fallows created and manufactured his own designs of tinplate toys. Ironically, his business began to fade around 1890—just about the time that lithographed toys were finally beginning to gain popularity.

Above: The Columbia, a rare tinplate paddle wheel floor toy, circa 1880s, features simple stenciled designs and embossed half circles. **Right:** A tinplate train engine, circa 1880s, has ornate tin embossing on the smoke stack and is stenciled "Flash" on the boiler.

Top left: This tinplate platform bell toy features an elephant. Top right: A hand-painted elephant is also the subject of this tinplate hoop toy. Above left (1): Fallows made this hand-painted tin horse-drawn fire pumper circa 1880. Above left: (2): While the company was well-known for its transportation toys, Fallows also made simple tinplate bell toys like this one depicting a lamb. Left: This tinplate "Jupiter" locomotive and tender are circa 1890s.

J. K. Farnell
London, England
1840 - 1968

John Farnell established this company in the Notting Hill section of London in 1840. The company started out by manufacturing pincushions and progressed to developing a variety of soft toys. After John's death in 1897, his children, Agnes and Henry, took over the business and moved it to Acton, in west London.

The company continued to grow, producing cloth dolls and, eventually, teddy bears of high quality. The teddy bear craze was in full swing during the 1920s, and companies around the world responded to the demand by manufacturing bruins. Farnell bears were all the rage at London's famous department store Harrods, where A.A. Milne, author of *Winnie the Pooh*, is believed to have been inspired to write his popular children's story by the Farnell bear he bought for his son Christopher in 1921. By the 1930s the company registered the trademark of "Alpha Toys," which they placed on every doll and bear manufactured. Some of Farnell's bears from the 1920s and early 1930s resemble Steiff bears, with their humped backs, long tapering arms and realistic muzzles. Like teddy bears by Steiff and Bing, Farnell mohair teddies from that era have a seam down the center of the chest.

The company also produced a range of cloth dolls, often felt or velvet. Its best-known dolls were a set representing the coronation of George VI in 1937. Like the teddy bears, the dolls also had cloth labels on the soles of their feet. Even though the factory was destroyed by fire in the mid-1930s and bombed in the 1940s, Farnell continued to produce well-made toys through 1968.

Above: These two glass-eyed Farnell teddy bears are both circa 1930s. The one at left is 18 inches with long silky pale-gold mohair, web-stitched claws and felt paw pads, while the one at right, in slightly better condition, is 22 inches, with blond mohair and linen pads.

Fisher-Price
East Aurora, New York
1930

isher-Price began operations on October 1, 1930, in East Aurora, New York. The founders of the company, Herman Fisher and Irving Price, met through mutual friends to create a major American toy manufacturing company. At the time of their meeting, Herman Fisher worked for All-Fair Toys, a producer of board games, which was having problems. Fisher had tried, unsuccessfully, to buy out the company. Irving Price had a sound management experience at F.W. Woolworth Co. The two com-

bined forces with Helen M. Schelle who, at the time, ran the Walker Toy Shop in Binghamton, New York. In addition to possessing an incredible eye for children's toys, she had developed extensive contacts with buyers in New York City. She became the first secretary and treasurer of the Fisher-Price toy company. Margaret Price, a writer and illustrator for Rand McNally, Harper & Brothers and Strecher Lithography, became the first artist and designer for the new company. Her attention to detail and use

Identification Clues

- All Fisher-Price toys are marked somewhere on the toy with the company logo and product number

- If the piece is all wood, it was produced from 1931 – 1949. Plastic was introduced in the 1950s and by 1964 plastic had completely replaced wood in the production of Fisher-Price toys.

Above: The wooden #141 Snap-Quack realistic Mallard Duck was designed by nationally known wildlife artist Lynn Bogue, circa late 1940s. **Left:** Fisher-Price used this logo and numbering system on its toys from the 1930s to the 1940s.

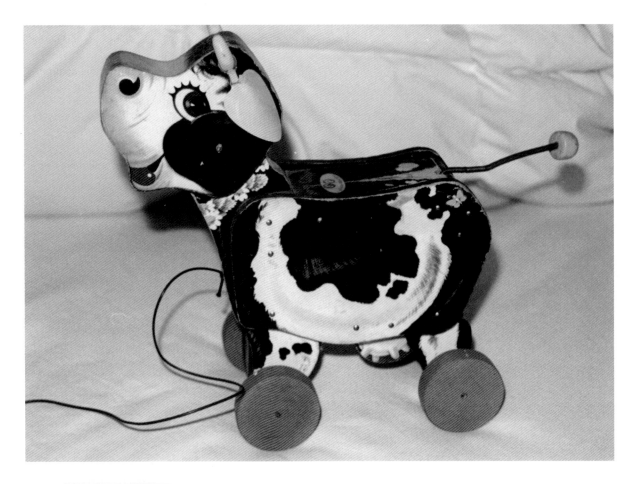

Collector Alert

The most desirable and hardest-to-find pieces are pre-World-War-II, all-wood characters. The more plastic used in the production of a Fisher-Price toy, the lower its value.

of vibrant colors set the toys apart from the others being produced during this time period.

This new team worked hard to bring the "Sixteen Hopefuls"–the inaugural Fisher-Price toy line–to market. Among their debut toys were Granny Doodle, Barky Puppy and the whimsical Woodsy-Wee Zoo. The company established five criteria for the production of their toys: intrinsic play value; ingenuity; strong construction; good value for the money; action. Once their solid foundation had been established, the company took the manufacturing world by storm. The colors and sturdiness of the toys amazed and delighted children everywhere. The first shipment was delivered to Macy's in New York City. By the

end of 1931, more than seven hundred stores carried Fisher-Price toys. The line continued to grow, with comic characters like Popeye, Mickey Mouse and Donald Duck being added to production.

As the years passed, the company incorporated pull toys, push toys and educational toys. The action of the toy, or the noise it produced, always seemed to attract children. Collectors still look for the vibrant colors that may remain on the lithographed paper and take special note to see if the "action" aspect of the toy is still functional. Most toys have experienced significant playwear because they were durable enough to pass from sibling to sibling. Fisher-Price remains one of the strongest children's toy companies today.

Above: In the 1950s, Fisher-Price began to combine plastic with wood, as seen on the #155 Moo-oo Cow. **Above left:** The logo on the Moo-oo Cow is the typical one used by the company in the mid 1950s.

Top left: In the 1950s, Fisher-Price was still making paper-on-wood pull toys, like this #777 Squeaky the Clown and the #140 Katy Kackler, left. **Above:** This detail shot shows the use of the logo and numbering system on Katy Kackler.

Above: The #476 Mickey Mouse Drummer has moveable wooden arms and mallets that beat his metal-topped drum, which is on a wooden base with wooden wheels. The toy dates from 1941. **Right:** The close-up photo shows the logo and numbering system used by Fisher-Price.

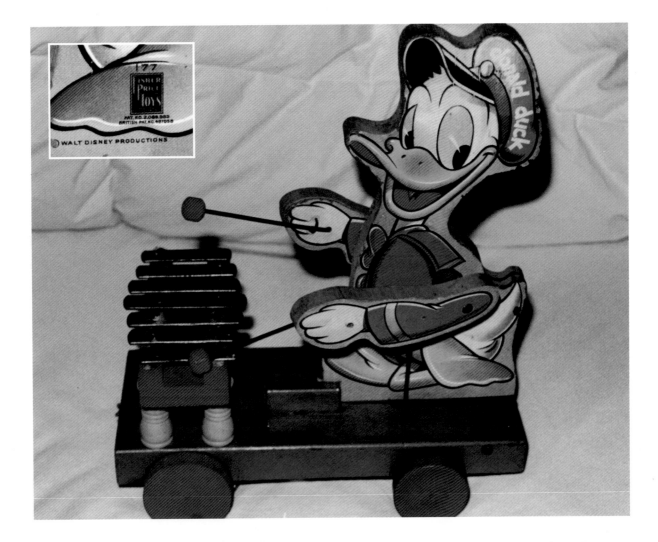

Top: The #177 Donald Duck xylophone player, circa 1946, has moveable wooden arms, metal keys and a wooden base with wooden wheels. **Above:** This #705 Popeye Cowboy wooden pull toy is circa 1937. **Left:** The #780 Jumbo xylophone player also dates from 1937.

Francis Field & Francis
Philadelphia, Pennsylvania
1838 - 1850s

Top, above and right: This company produced toys of steel plated with tin and hand painted. Decorative detailing was originally added by hand, but eventually a stenciling process was used instead.

This company holds the distinction of being one of the oldest American toy manufacturers on record. Established around 1838, it was also known as the Philadelphia Tin Toy Manufactory. This company toy-making system involved assembling the toy in stages. The sections of steel plated with tin were pressed out under great pressure, shaped and then soldered or tabbed together. The entire piece was finished off with a hand-applied coat of paint. Once that dried, decorative detailing was also done by hand. Later, the stenciling process replaced the freehand details. The company produced horse-drawn wagons and carriages; horses, dogs and cows on wheeled platforms; wheeled boats; dollhouse furniture; bell toys; locomotives; and figures of a boy seated on a dog with a flag. James Fallows, an English immigrant, worked as a foreman for the company perfecting the craft of tin toy manufacturing before leaving the company to start his own toy company in 1874.

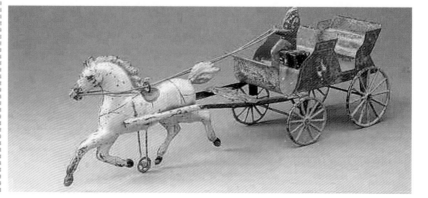

Georgene Novelties Company
New York, New York
1920 - 1962

Founded in about 1920 by Georgene Averill, this company holds the distinction of manufacturing Raggedy Ann and Raggedy Andy dolls over the course of more years than any other company in the twentieth century. While best known for Raggedy Ann, this company also designed a French girl doll; Gypsy Queen; Lucky Rastus; Romper Boy; and Toto the Clown; as well as Birthday Dolls (with the flowers for each month) for George Borgfeldt in 1927. A cloth doll designed by Maude Tousy Fangel, known as Sweets, was distributed as a Georgene doll. But it was Raggedy Ann that made the name of Georgene well known in the doll world.

To better understand the phenomenon of Raggedy Ann, we have to take a closer look at her creator, Johnny B. Gruelle. Gruelle was born in Arcola, Illinois, in 1880 and grew up to become a political cartoonist for the *Indianapolis Star* and, later, for the *New York Herald*. In 1915, while he was working at the *Star*, his daughter Marcella fell seriously ill. In an effort to entertain and comfort his daughter, Gruelle found an old rag doll in the attic. He named it Raggedy Ann and presented it to Marcella, who not only enjoyed the cloth doll but also the stories her father made up about the adventures of Raggedy Ann. Sadly, Marcella died a year later, but the stories lived on in the books chronicling Raggedy Ann's adventures that Gruelle went on to publish.

Gruelle patented the doll image

Above: Georgene manufactured Raggedy Ann and Raggedy Andy beginning in 1938 until 1962. During that time the dolls underwent numerous design transitions. These two examples, most likely dating from the 1940s, feature the traditionally recognized striped legs and sewn-on cotton wigs. Andy's white collar, which began to be used in the early 1940s is a clue to his date.

Identification Clues

- Early dolls have shoe-button eyes sewn on through the head; dolls made in 1950s have tin button eyes attached with two prongs

- Early dolls have wool wigs; after mid 1940s wigs are cotton

- Early Georgene dolls have black outline around a long triangular red nose; over the years it evolved into a small orange triangle with no outline

- Tag stating " Johnny Gruelle's Own Raggedy Ann & Andy Dolls" and Georgene Novelties, Inc., Exclusive Licensed Manufacturers" as well as trademark, copyright and patent information is sewn into the doll's left side seam

- Very earliest Georgene Raggedy Ann & Andy dolls each had their own tag: Ann was printed in red and Andy was printed in blue

Above: This Raggedy Ann also dates from the 1940s. The "I Love You" heart was always printed on the body, although the very earliest dolls made by the Gruelle family had actual candy hearts bearing the phrase inserted into the dolls' chests.

and the book in 1915. The Gruelle family made the original dolls under his direction until 1918, when the P.F. Volland Co. took over production of the books as well as of Raggedy Ann and Raggedy Andy dolls. Eventually that company also made Beloved Belindy and many other characters from the stories.

By 1935, the Volland Company ceased to exist, and the manufacturing copyrights reverted to Johnny Gruelle, who sold them to the Exposition Doll Company. This company was only able to produce the dolls for about a year, and meanwhile non-coyrighted versions were produced by American Toy and Novelty. Although Gruelle was the rightful copyright owner, in 1935 Mollye's Doll Outfitters applied for and received a patent to produce Raggedy

Ann and Andy. Gruelle fought a three-year court battle, during which time Mollye's made millions of dolls.

By the time he won the lawsuit in 1938, Johnny Gruelle had died. His wife, Myrtle, awarded permission to Georgene Novelties Company Inc. to manufacture Raggedy Ann and Andy. In the 1940's the company expanded the line by adding an asleep-awake Raggedy Ann, and a Camel with Wrinkled Knees. Over the decades Georgene slowly adapted the dolls' design and production, as well as the tags, resulting in at least six different mouth shapes, five different eye designs, six different noses, and three versions of the "I Love You" heart, which was printed on the body. In 1962, the Gruelle family gave the right to produce the dolls to Knickerbocker.

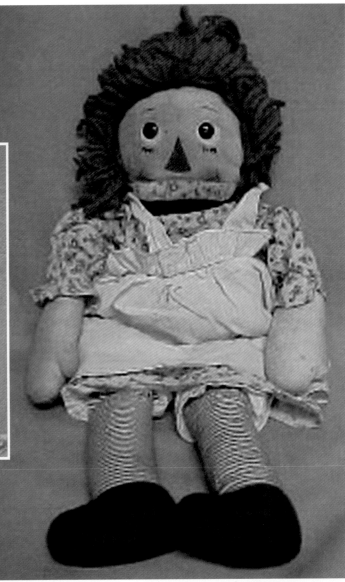

Above: By the mid 1940s the dolls' noses had lost their black outlines and had more of a scoop to the shape. Both Ann and Andy, left, bore the same tag, authorizing Georgene as the exclusive licensed manufacturer, above.

Gibbs Manufacturing Company
Canton, Ohio
1884 - 1969

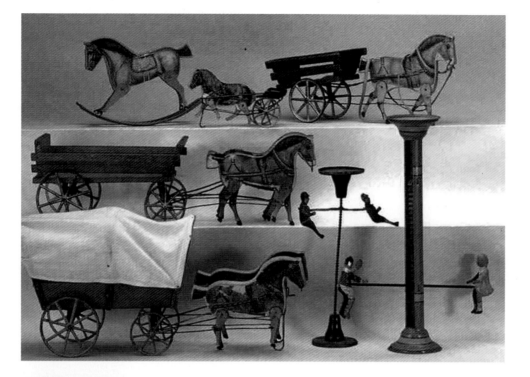

Top and above: Gibbs was known especially for its toys with motion and action. Toys produced in the 1920s included horse-drawn vehicles as well as toys activated by gravity, such as the piece above. Children were especially drawn to the movable features of the horse-drawn toys.

While Connecticut was the cradle of early toy manufacturers, Ohio has proven to be home of some enduring and durable toy companies that were founded in the second half of the 1800s and well into the twentieth century. The Gibbs Manufacturing Company was founded by Lewis E. Gibbs, who established his company in 1830 with the production of wooden barrels and tubs, later adding rakes and hardware specialties to his line. As a child, Gibbs had worked for his father, Joshua Gibbs, who was an inventor and plow manufacturer. Farm equipment, particularly plows, were very popular throughout the Ohio farmlands as well as across the Great Plains, and the advances Gibbs introduced in the production of metal plows were warmly welcomed by farmers throughout the Midwest.

Gibbs was unexpectedly thrust into the toy business and the national political arena when William McKinley's campaign manager contacted him with the request to create a political giveaway. McKinley was from Canton, Ohio, and the idea of a hometown businessman creating a novelty for the Presidential candidate virtually assured a successful campaign run. Gibbs was flattered, and

rose to the occasion by manufacturing a spring-driven top that featured pictures of McKinley and his running mate, along with the slogan "McKinley on Top" and "I Spin For McKinley."

Due to the success of the toy top, the company continued to manufacture toys with motion and action. These included push-and-pull toys; animals that pulled various wagons and carts featuring legs that moved; an Irishman dancing a jig; and a cat with a bobbing head. The company developed the slogan, "You have only to put Gibbs toys on your counters and they sell themselves." The toys were attractive, and children enjoyed the motion of the tops and the movable features of the horse-drawn toys and floor toys.

Gibbs continued to run the company until his death in 1914. His sons and other family members continued to efficiently run the company, expanding the line to include advertising toys to order and lithographed paper-on-wood toys. The extensive toy line coupled with competitive pricing (prices ranged from one to thirty-five cents), helped sustain the company through the lean depression years. The Gibbs Manufacturing Company continued toy production until 1969.

A. C. Gilbert Company
New Haven, Connecticut
1908 - 1966

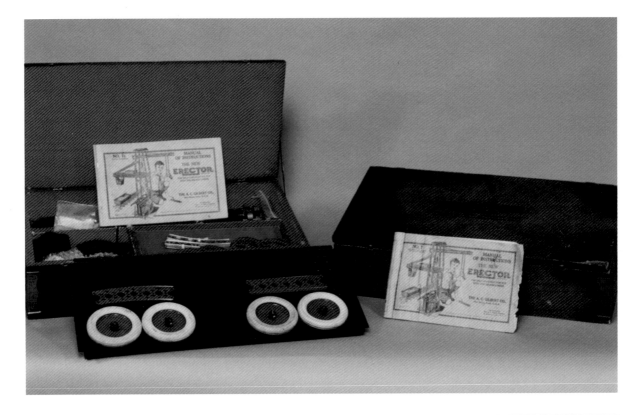

The founder of this company, Alfred Carlton Gilbert, was born in 1884 into a family that can trace its genealogy back to the Elizabethan explorer, Sir Humphrey Gilbert. In 1904, Glbert entered Yale University Medical School. To help support himself financially, he performed magic shows locally. He delayed his graduation so he could participate in the London Olympics in 1908, where he won a gold medal, but never returned to competitive sports.

With his gold medal in hand, Gilbert returned to Yale and established the Mysto Magic Company in 1908. He took on a partner, John Petrie, a local resident and machinist who also had an interest in magic and manufactured magic props. By 1909 the magical duo were manufacturing boxed sets of magic equipment for the wholesale trade. This was also the year that Gilbert graduated from Yale and began to devote all of his time to sales and promotion. Petrie continued to produce the magic sets for their grow- ing new business. In 1911, Gilbert bought out Petrie and changed the direction of the company.

In spite of his degree from Yale Medical School, Gilbert turned his sights toward engineering and con- struction. He introduced his new line of Erector Sets, priced from $1 to $25, at the Toy Fairs in 1913, and they were an instant success. Gilbert's new cre- ation was a miniature reflection of American society, which was experi- encing a boom in construction. The Erector Sets were the first American construction toy with moving parts and motors. His new line was awarded with the gold medal at the Panama Pacific Exposition. Over the next forty years, more than thirty million Erector Sets would be sold.

Much of Gilbert's early success was due to an enormous amount of advertising in national magazines. He knew the value of vast exposure for your product. This media blitz began in 1913. The next three years proved profitable, and by 1916 the company

Top: This example of Gilbert's famous Erector Set has its original box and instructions. **Above:** Gilbert's story was told in this undated magazine article detailing his story, and describ- ing him as Toy King.

experienced some major changes. The name was officially changed to the A.C. Gilbert Company and the entire business was brought together to occupy a five-block square in New Haven, Connecticut, fondly known as Erector Square. By this time Gilbert held close to one hundred and fifty patents for his creations.

Being the consummate businessman, he knew his line must keep up with the changes in America. So, in 1914, he developed a line of pressed steel automobiles and trucks. In addition, after World War I, the company began manufacturing a line of scientific toys with a high degree of educational value. In 1916 Gilbert estab-

lished the Toy Manufacturers of America (TMA). He became the first president, setting its main objective to further the interests of American toy manufacturers as a result of the embargo on German products after the war in Europe.

By 1938, Gilbert decided to take over the financially strapped American Flyer Corporation. He relocated the entire operation from Chicago to New Haven, redesigned the look and packaging of the trains, and retained the well-known American Flyer name. Gilbert's magic helped revive American Flyer's sales to be competitive with Lionel trains.

Above: Gilbert's boxed erector locomotive and tender set was one of the company's popular items, as were the carpenter's tools featured in the 1920 advertisement, left.

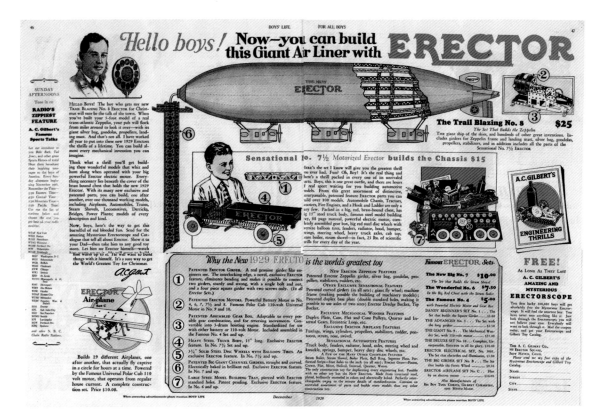

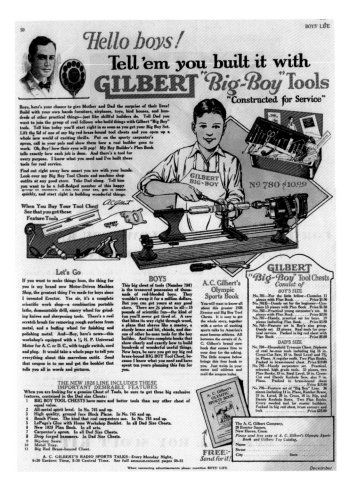

Collector Alert

The most desirable to collectors are sets intact with all the pieces in good condition. If pieces are lacking, or the box is missing, the value is significantly reduced.

Gilbert understood the value of media exposure and advertised heavily in magazines published for children. The advertising on these pages featured the Big-Boy Tools set in *Boy's Life* in December 1928 and a variety of transportation toys in the same magazine a year later, in December 1929.

Girard Manufacturing Company
Girard, Pennsylvania
1919 - 1935

Above: The focus of Frank E. Wood's Girard Manufacturing Company was pressed-steel clockwork automobiles and trucks. The Fire Chief vehicle is a typical car design by Girard.

When Frank E. Wood established The Toy Works in Girard, Pennsylvania, and manufactured his first toys, his company's headliner was a walking porter pushing a wheelbarrow. The line also featured spinning tops, skates and banks. The toys were a success, but the following year a fire destroyed the warehouse and all its contents.

The company regrouped and reorganized its product line. The name was changed to the Girard Model Works and the focus became pressed-steel clockwork automobiles and trucks, as well as mechanical tin toys. To help stimulate business during this rebuilding period, the company sub-contracted toys to order for Ferdinand Strauss and the giant in the toy industry, Louis Marx. The demand placed on the manufacturing company during this period resulted in a greater quantity of toys produced for other companies with their logos and fewer toys produced with the Girard motto: "Making childhood's hour happier."

The toy manufacturing business was maturing quickly and New York City became the capital of corporate sales. Frank Wood added a sales office in the building on Fifth Avenue located in the heart of the toy district. He continued to run the company until the end of the 1920s. In 1928 the company was taken over by a stock company of investors and in 1929 the Girard Model Works secured a five-year deal with Louis Marx, making him a commission agent.

For the next few years the company produced toys with the Marx-Girard label, and prospered. Girard Model Works grew to accommodate the increase in production, and by the end of 1930 the company occupied twenty-three buildings in three surrounding communities. The company found its target audience by selling their toys priced between ten cents and one dollar, through chain stores and mail-order houses. Louis Marx had a vested interest in the company and became the major stockholder.

In 1934, Girard's contract with Marx expired and was not renewed. This did not sit well with Louis Marx, as the Girard Model Works was responsible for the development and production of his trains and pressed steel automobiles, which were dominating the toy market at this time. Marx rallied the other stockholders to pursue legal action to take control of Girard which forced bankruptcy. The reorganization of the company was complete in 1935, with Louis Marx and his brother David named as directors of the Girard Manufacturing Company. The company continued to take direction from Marx in New York, who maintained a controlling interest.

From top: The design of this car is the same as that of the Fire Chief vehicle on the opposite page, though the color is different. Toy companies often produced the same design in a variety of colors. Girard's mechanical airplane, shown here with its original box, was promoted for its sturdiness as well as its realistic appearance.

Gong Bell Manufacturing Company
East Hampton, Connecticut
1866 - 1960s

This company achieved great popularity with the production of cast-iron bell-toys. First patented in 1874, bell toys became an American phenomenon; they combined a wheeled base with a bell that rang when the toy was pushed or pulled. William Barton, a blacksmith and entrepreneur who had established the East Hampton, Connecticut, base for production of household items in 1808, can be credited with developing the technique for casting bells in one piece, as opposed to the European method in which two pieces were soldered together. The Barton one-piece bell was both stronger and less expensive to produce. In 1837 his company became the Hampton Bell Company, and in 1866 the name was changed to the Gong Bell Company. The company perfected the manufacturing techniques and experimented with the design, easily establishing itself as the market leader. In addition to bell toys, the company also produced hand bells, sleigh bells and doorbells.

The bell toy delighted children for hours. The pull toys were skillfully designed with the bells incorporated into the design. One featured a bell placed under the toy; as it traveled across the floor a small hammer attached to the axle struck the bell. Another showcased the bells attached to a figure on the toy, which shook as the toy was pulled. On yet another the figure would strike the bell as the toy was pulled. A variety of bell sizes provided a different sound for each toy.

The J. & E. Stevens Company, located in neighboring Cromwell, Connecticut, produced the wheels for the Gong Bell toys. One was a very elaborate and ornate wheel that complemented the toys especially well.

The cast-iron pull toys manufactured by Gong Bell at the turn of the century are quite desirable and collectible today. The beauty and simplicity of the cast-iron figures and bells continue to captivate the imagination.

Half size Cut No. 10.

TUMBLER BELL TOYS, with horses.

No. 10, ... per dozen, $1.15
" 11, ... "   3.75

Above: The Gong Bell Manufacturing Company's success was based upon its popular cast-iron bell toys, such as Jonah and the Whale and a clown in a pig cart, both of which were produced in the 1880s. **Left:** A page from the company's catalog illustrates the horse-drawn tumbler bell toys.

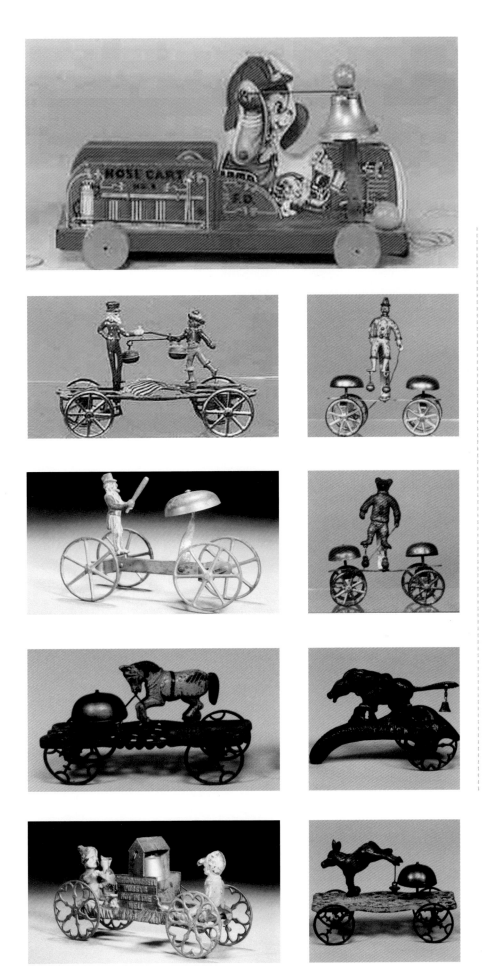

Collector Alert

The cast-iron bell toys have been reproduced from a cast iron of lesser quality. The originals are distinguished by a high quality of paint, smooth cast iron and an active bell device.

The toys on this page showcase the diversity of toys made by Gong Bell during its years of production. The paper-on-wood fire toy, top, is a later piece, while the others are earlier cast-iron bell toys. Several different designs incorporated the bells into the pull toys, and a variety of bell sizes provided different sounds for each toy.

Gund

Edison, New Jersey
1898

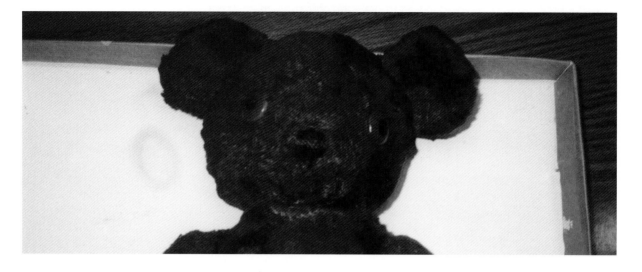

Identification Clues

- No tags on bears or toys prior to 1940s

- From 1940 to World War II, tags read "A Gund Product, A Toy of Quality and Distinction"

- After 1948 a stylized "G" appears as a rabbit with ears and whiskers

- If the label shows a New York City address the bear was produced between 1940 – 1956

- In 1956 the factory moved to Brooklyn, NY, and the tags reflected this address through 1973

This company is one of the oldest American stuffed toy manufacturers that is still in business, and still run by descendants of an original employee of the company. The company was founded by Adolph Gund in 1898 in Norwalk, Connecticut, and began manufacturing belts, necklaces, novelties and handmade stuffed toys. In 1906 Gund purchased some plush and began producing bears in four sizes, ranging from ten to sixteen inches. He followed up with rabbits for Easter, and experimented with other animals. In 1907 the company moved to New York City. In 1910 his company incorporated and presented its first line of stuffed animals. The public response was overwhelming, so the company continued to focus production on stuffed toy animals. As the company grew, Gund hired Jacob Swedlin as a janitor in 1919. Swedlin was the oldest of seven children and took the job to help support his family, newly arrived from Russia in the United States. His hard work and determination resulted in a promotion to the cutting department. Within three years Swedlin was head of the cutting department and soon Adolph Gund selected him to be his personal assistant. This promotion provided Swedlin the necessary exposure to the everyday running of the Gund Corporation.

After twenty-seven years of business, the original Gund Corporation was dissolved in 1925 and the assets of the company were taken over by Swedlin. The company became known as Gund Manufacturing Company, Jacob Swedlin, Inc. Swedlin and two brothers, Abraham and Louis, reorganized the company and continued to revolutionize the industry. Swedlin is credited with developing the use of machines to accurately and more efficiently cut the patterns for the stuffed toys. Gund was also the first to utilize foam rubber and synthetic materials into the designs of their stuffed toys. Today, the privately held company, now based in Edison, New Jersey, is still owned and run by descendants of Jacob Swedlin, who continue to create bears and stuffed toys that are prized by children and collectors alike.

Above: This early example of a Gund bear has the characteristic eyes and round cupped ears that the company used in the production of bears during the 1920s. **Left:** A later publicity photo, dated 1961, features a young boy with the perennially popular rabbits Gund has produced throughout most of its history.

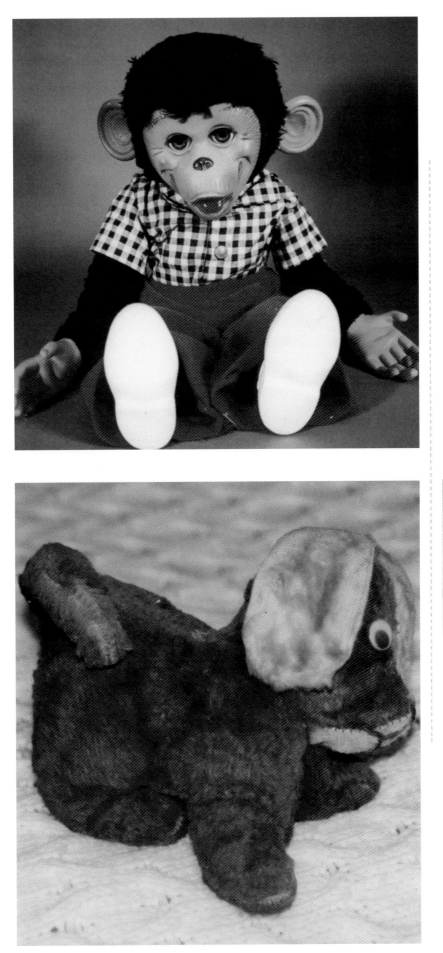

Top left: Gund was known for innovations such as using a combination of materials on animals, as shown on this monkey, which has a cloth body and a plastic face. **Left:** This plush puppy has the typical googly eyes the company used on its bears and animals in the 1920s and 1930s.

Hafner Manufacturing Company
Chicago, Illinois
1900 - 1950

William Hafner began his business in Chicago in 1900 as the Toy Auto Company, and by 1907 he had a line of seven different clockwork wind-up motorized vehicles. In 1904 the company became the W. F. Hafner Company, evolved into the American Train Company and then, in 1910, became the American Flyer company.

Hafner was not interested in branching out his business, so in 1914 he broke away from American Flyer. He and his son, who had recently been discharged from the Navy, formed the Hafner Manufacturing Company. They produced wind-up trains until 1951, when Hafner sold

his company to All Metal, which produced Wyandotte's toys.

All of the trains manufactured by Hafner were clockwork-mechanism wind-ups, that were O gauge in scale. The gauge of toy trains determined the type of track that the train would run on, as well as the size of the other cars and accessories that were needed to supplement sets. The gauge is determined by the measurement of space between the inside rails of the track, or the space between the wheels of the toy. O gauge measures 1¼ inches, while standard guage measures 2 1/8 inches. The popular HO guage measures 5/8 of an inch.

Above: William Hafner's company went through a variety of name changes, but he always wanted to focus on producing vehicles that could actually move, such as the circa-1930s trains on this page. All of these are wind-up trains with clockwork mechanisms and tinplate cars.

Heinrich Handwerck
Waltershausen, Germany
1876 - 1932

Collector Alert

This area of doll collecting is vast, as there were many German bisque-doll manufacturers, who often made parts for each other. Identification can be tricky for the beginning collector, who is advised to consult some of the many doll guides that exist.

This German manufacturer's dolls had standard composition ball-jointed bodies with bisque heads made by Simon & Halbig from Handwerck's molds and marked Handwerck. The dolls had human or mohair hair, depending on the quality of the doll being produced.

After Handwerck's death in 1902, his company was taken over by Kämmer & Reinhardt, but use of the Handwerck name continued. The dolls were sold by Gimbel's, Macy's and Montgomery Ward. By this time, some of the dolls had sleep eyes and, like many dolls of the era, were often sold wearing only chemises.

The firm closed in 1918 and was resurrected in the early 1920s under the ownership of Heinrich Handwerck Jr., the founder's son. He moved the facilities to Gotha and continued to manufacture ball-jointed dolls until the company closed its doors in 1932.

Identification Clues

- Bisque heads incised on the back of the head with numbers that represent the mold # or no number at all but incised:

  HANDWERK
  Germany
  — OR —
  Germany
  HEINRICH HANDWERK
  SIMON & HALBIG

Above: Typical of this popular German manufacturer's production is the bisque-headed child on a composition body. This example features an open mouth and paperweight eyes.

Hermann
Sonneberg, Germany
1907

Identification Clues

- Bears by Max Hermann often had a printed paper tag featuring a bear and running dog with the words Maheso
- Bears by Bernhard Hermann had a swing tag that read: Marke Beha Teddy Burgt Fur Qualitat

Above: The Gebrüder Hermann company produced a Zotty-type bear in the 1950s and 1960s. This fully jointed mohair example has an outlined open mouth. While Steiff was first to produce a Zotty in 1951, the Hermann Zotty does not have the white colored chest plate of the Steiff examples.

Next to Steiff, the Hermann name is probably most widely identified with early German teddy bears. Today there are two distinct companies with that name making teddy bears of high quality in Germany: Gebrüder Hermann GmbH & Co, KG and Hermann-Spielwaren GmbH. The two companies are owned by distant cousins descended from Johann Hermann, who started a toy company at Neufang, near Sonneberg, Germany, in 1907 and made his first teddy bear in 1913. Johann had six children, and all were somehow involved in the teddy bear industry. After Johann's death in 1919, his second son, Artur, moved to Sonneberg and continued to make soft animals, including teddy bears. He moved to Munich in 1940 and sold the business in 1954 to the Anker Plush Toy Company.

Johann's eldest son, Bernhard, eventually started his own business making teddy bears and dolls, also in Sonneberg and, after World War II, established a factory in Hirschaid, in the US Zone. His four sons were all instrumental in the business, which became known as Gebrüder Hermann (Hermann Brothers) and is still in operation today, under the direction of Bernhard's granddaughters.

Another son of Johann's, Max, stayed in Neufang and founded his own toy firm in 1920, which he eventually moved to Sonneberg. In 1947 his son Rolf-Gerhard joined his firm and in 1949 Max and Rolf-Gerhard founded Hermann & Co. KG in Coburg, which much later, in 1979, became Hermann-Spielwaren GmbH, and which is still run today by Rolf-Gerhard and his daughter Ursula.

All the Hermann firms produced traditional-looking mohair bears of fine quality, which can often be identified by their inset, contrasting muzzles.

Bears made by Hermann are often distinguished by an oversized inset muzzle of short-pile mohair, as seen on this example.

N. N. Hill Brass Company
East Hampton, Connecticut
1889 - 1960

Identification Clues

- Early bell toys were not marked, difficult to positively identify
- The company used wheels from other companies, adding to the difficulty of identification

This company established itself as a major manufacturer of cast-iron bell toys and cornered the market, both in quality of design as well as quantity produced. Between the years of 1903 and 1907 the company operated as a branch of the National Novelty Corporation. In 1905, after National acquired the Watrous Manufacturing Company, the parent company decided to combine Watrous and the Hill Brass Company. The bell toys made after this date were produced in cast iron and pressed steel with a bell incorporated into every design.

Top: Made circa the 1890s, the Banana Boys See-Saw is a cast-iron bell toy. **Above:** Monkeys were a favorite subject for children's toys of the 1890s, as seen on this cast-iron bell toy. **Right:** The N. N. Hill Brass Company was one of many to interpret the popular story of Jonah and the Whale as a toy.

Recognized as the oldest American doll company, Horsman was started by German-born Edward Imeson Horsman as a toy importer in 1865. Records show that by 1878 he had expanded to assembling toys, including dolls. The logical next step was to begin manufacturing dolls, which he did around the turn of the century. Some of the first known Horsman dolls were cloth with hand-painted faces, such as the Babyland Rag dolls. By 1907 the faces began to be printed on the dolls and by 1909 Horsman gave them celluloid faces. Eventually he turned to composition, calling the dolls made from this durable material Can't Break 'Em. One of the first in this group was the character known as

Billiken, for which Horsman obtained a copyright in 1909.

The success of Billiken led Horsman to create more character dolls, such as Baby Bumps, the Campbell Kids and, in the 1920s, film characters such as Little Mary Mix-Up and Jackie Coogan as The Kid. The Horsman Art Dolls appeared in 1911 in three sizes ranging from 10½ to 15½ inches. Designers of the dolls included Helen Trowbridge and Bernard Lipfert.

The Aetna Doll Company made the composition heads for Horsman and the two companies merged in 1918 to be the E. I. Horsman & Aetna Co., but later returned to being known simply as E. I. Horsman Co. The company produced affordable

Identification Clues

- Usually marked on back of head or shoulder
- Used a variety of marks, including full name or E.I.H.Co.
- Early composition dolls marked "Can't Break 'Em"
- Horsman reproduced early dolls in vinyl in the 1980s

Above: Horsman began to produce the walking/talking child dolls known as Rosebud circa 1915-1920. This 20-inch example is marked Rosebud on the back of her composition socket head, and has tin sleep eyes, a human-hair wig and cloth torso.

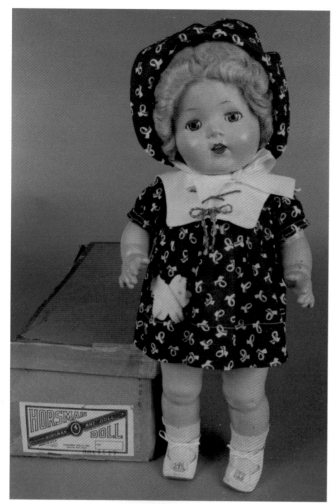

Top left: This 18-inch toddler is shown with her original box. The label on the box reads "Horsman Doll, Genuine Horsman Art Doll, Made in U.S.A., Horsman Dolls Inc., Trenton, New Jersey." **Top right:** Horsman produced the Campbell Kids, inspired by the Campbell Soup drawings, in a wide variety of national costumes, beginning in about 1912. This 13-inch Indian Girl is composition and marked E.I.H.Co. INC on the back of her head. Her clothing is still tagged with a label reading: Horsman Doll, Made in U.S.A. **Above:** Among the earliest dolls produced by Horsman (and most likely made by Bruckner for the company) were the Babyland Rag dolls. This 14-inch example is marked Pat'd. July 9th 1901 at the bottom of her pressed cloth mask face.

play dolls throughout the century, including a wide variety of baby dolls, walking/talking Mama dolls and characters such as Ella Cinders and the HEbee-SHEbee dolls. In the 1980s the company began to reproduce some of its own early successes in vinyl, but these are always well-marked as replicas. Though Edward Horsman died in 1927, the company has endured through various owners and today Horsman Ltd. is based in Great Neck, New York.

Hubley Manufacturing Company
Lancaster, Pennsylvania
1894

I n 1894, John E. Hubley, working with a group of investers, had a factory built to produce toy trains and parts in Lancaster, Pennsylvania. The invention of electricity had revolutionized modern society and was now entering toy manufacturing. Hubley recognized that his novel toys that ran on electricity would stand out from the cast-iron floor trains and clockwork mechanisms already on the market. With this in mind the company's motto became: "They're Different."

The toy manufacturing company found quick success, which continued well into the twentieth century until stopped by a tragic factory fire in 1909. In search of a new site, Hubley found the abandoned Safety Buggy Company factory and set up shop there. The destruction of the entire line of toys in addition to moving costs and start-up expenses of a new facility took its toll on the Hubley Manufacturing Company. John H. Hartman and Joseph T. Breneman came to the rescue by putting together a group of investors who purchased the company.

The Hubley Manufacturing Company received its biggest break from Butler Brothers, the nation's largest wholesaler jobber, which placed huge orders. These orders helped changed the focus of the company from the original line to cast-iron toys, hardware and novelties. The first toys were horse-drawn wagons; fire engines; miniature coal stoves; circus trains; and toy guns. Hubley was also filling orders from other toy manufacturing companies. Ironically, as the company housed in an old buggy factory continued to grow, the item that domi-

Above: Among the earliest of the cast-iron toys made by Hubley were horse-drawn open carriages such as this example of an 1890s phaeton. **Left:** This cast-iron "static" racing boat pull toy illustrates some of the creative designs the company used for its cast-iron toys.

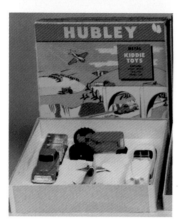

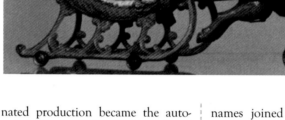

nated production became the automobile. In the 1930s, Hubley echoed the designs of popular full-size automobile in its toys.

The company's new direction of toy manufacturing proved very successful. They recognized the importance of offering the buying public affordable toys. In addition to expensive toys (priced from one to three dollars), Hubley also included nickel, dime and quarter toys in their production line. The company soon began to branch out by aligning toy production with popular manufacturers of the day. Soon consumers were seeing a Hubley toy Bell Telephone truck or a Hubley Packard toy car. Other brand names joined the roster, including Borden's, Old Dutch, General Electric and Maytag. This experiment paid off handsomely for Hubley as well as providing advertising for the other companies that participated.

The Hubley toys were educational, with functioning, realistic parts. Dump trucks dumped; grasshoppers had realistic legs; toys could be taken apart and put back together. World War II halted production of cast-iron toys and Hubley responded by changing to die-cast metal. In 1965 the company was bought by Gabriel Industrier and continues to make die-cast zinc and plastic toys.

Hubley manufactured a wide range of toys, as illustrated on this page. From a cast-iron water skier to reindeer-drawn sleighs and a realistic-looking Daddy Long Legs, as well as boxed sets of Kiddie Toys, the company's offerings were educational and functioning.

Collector Alert

Carefully inspect the cast-iron pieces for flaws, repairs or repainting and make sure the item is not a reproduction.

From top: The traveling circus in America influenced Hubley in the production of horse-drawn cast-iron toys. Among its horse-drawn toys was this coal wagon. **Left:** In this close-up view, the potential movement of the Daddy Long Legs pull toy is clear.

Top: When motorcycles captured America's fascination, Hubley quickly replicated the vehicles in cast iron for children. **Above:** The company's diverse range of subjects included this cast-iron surfer. The company usually cast its name right into the toy. **Above right and right:** This cast-iron "America" pull toy has three propellers.

Ideal Toy & Novelty Company
Brooklyn, New York
1903

The company was founded in Brooklyn, New York, by inventor Morris Michtom and his wife Rose, Russian immigrants who took special note of President Roosevelt's refusal to shoot a bear cub on a Mississippi hunt. After a cartoon by Clifford Berryman ran in the *Washington Post* entitled "Drawing the Line in Mississippi," which referred to Roosevelt's levelheaded attempt to settle a border dispute between Alabama and Mississippi, Rose hand crafted soft, jointed versions of the bear from the cartoon and displayed them in their storefront window. Soon this jointed bear became a favorite of the local community and The Ideal Novelty & Toy Company was formed to handle production to meet the over-whelming demand for the bears. Referring to the bear as Teddy's Bear, Morris apparently wrote a letter to President Roosevelt for permission to use his name, "Teddy," for the advertising of their new product. The legend continues that the President wrote back to the Michtoms giving his blessing on the name, but expressing doubt that it would add anything to the stuffed toys' popularity. Eventually the "'s" was dropped and the world adopted the phrase teddy bear.

Teddy bears accounted for Ideal's main production for many years; the company earned the distinction of being the first American manufacturing company to mass-produce bears. By the 1930s comic character toys were becoming very popular and the

Identification Clues

- The large head with a triangular face is one of the keys to identifying early bears

- Nose are usually broad-cloth or horizontally stitched

- Bears made before World War I have shoe-button eyes; post-WWI bears have glass eyes

- Bears have barrel-shaped body with humped back, stuffed with excelsior

- 1920s bears feature longer bodies, shorter limbs, low-set ears pinched together

Above: Between 1934 and 1939, Ideal's dolls of Shirley Temple grossed more than six million dollars in sales for the company. The company made composition dolls in the famous movie star's image in a variety of sizes and costumes. Three examples are shown here; the doll on the right wears the 1934 costume from the celebrity's first movie, *Stand up and Cheer*.

company obtained the rights to produce characters like Mickey Mouse, Popeye and Dopey. In addition, composition, and later plastic, dolls were added to the product line.

There were no permanent labels placed on the bears, so exact identification of the early bears can be difficult. The bears were produced with a distinctive style of design that seasoned collectors have come to recognize. Dolls are usually marked on the back or under the hairline on the back of the neck. The toys, however, always have the logo and company name on the toy itself, or on the box in which they are packaged.

Above and right: A later favorite doll by Ideal was the plastic 16-inch Mary Hartline character, circa 1952. The majorette from the television show *Super Circus* is shown here with her original box and tags.

Behind The Scenes

We were doing appraisals for the *Antiques Roadshow* in Louisville, Kentucky, when a woman brought a copy of the book *More About Teddy B and Teddy G: The Roosevelt Bears* by Seymour Eaton, published in 1907, along with an early Ideal bear. She wanted to get some idea of the value of her bear and book. She also presented me with a photograph of her great-grandmother on Christmas with the bear and book in her lap. The old sepia-tone photograph was dated 1907, which corresponded with the inscription inside the book: "Elva M. Rabuck of Louisville, KY. Christmas 1907."

The bear featured beautiful short clipped mohair; cupped ears; shoe-button eyes; a cloth nose; a barrel-shaped body, a hump back; and a triangular-shaped head—all characteristics of the Ideal bears of the early twentieth century. The overall condition and desirability of the bear, book and photograph made the package tremendously attractive to any collector. My opinion of its value was $3,000-$3,500, which astounded the woman. She had found these items in an old trunk in the attic, while the house was being cleaned out after Elva's death. About a year after the appraisal the woman contacted me to help her sell the items. She felt it was time to let them go, and hoped a new collector would better appreciate their historic value. She sent me the bear, book and photograph and the entire package sold on-line in an internet auction through TreasureQuest Auction Galleries, Inc for $4,000.

Top left: This 1906 Ideal teddy bear, with its triangular head, cupped, wide-set ears and oval foot pads, is a classic example of the company's earliest bears. **Left:** This fine example of a 1907 Ideal fully jointed mohair bear features the characteristic nose and shoe-button eyes.

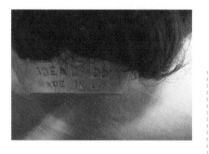

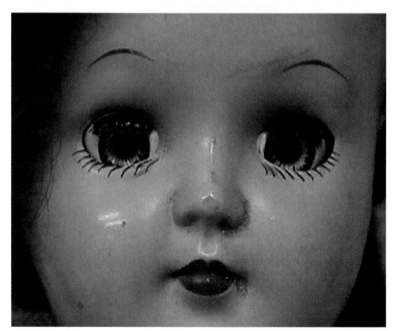

Top left: Ideal's composition version of the well-known entertainer Fanny Brice was popular circa 1937. Top right: The company's wide range of dolls included this composition soldier with molded hair, uniform and hat. Above: Ideal marked its dolls just below the hairline on the back of the neck. Right: The use of hard plastic for dolls allowed for a high level of detail in the face painting.

Ingersoll Watch Company
New York, New York
1880 - 1944

I n 1880 two young brothers from Michigan, twenty-one-year-old Robert and fifteen-year-old Charles, started the Ingersoll Watch Company in New York City. They created a pocket watch design and presented it to the Waterbury Clock Company, which agreed to produce twelve thousand pieces with a price tag of $1.50 each. The popularity of their design took off. Three years later the brothers designed another watch, which sold for one dollar each. By 1895 production of their watches had hit fifteen million.

By 1899, the brothers' pocket watch captured the attention of Symond's, a London shop, which placed a one-million order for the popular watch. This prompted a new advertising slogan, "Ingersoll—The watch that made the dollar famous." The success of the company continued into the new century, and in 1922 the Waterbury Clock Company bought out the Ingersoll brothers' company, which continued to do business using the name of Ingersoll—Waterbury Company.

A decade later the new company struck a deal with the Walt Disney company to produce a wrist watch featuring Mickey Mouse on the face and three little mice chasing each other on the second-hand dial. The watch came in a cardboard case bearing popular Disney characters of 1933 such as Mickey and Minnie Mouse, Pluto the Pup and Clarabelle cow. The watches were a huge success, and the company continued production, adding alarm clocks, until 1944. During this time period only Mickey Mouse, Donald Duck and the Big Bad Wolf and Three Little Pigs were featured on the watches.

Identification Clues

- In 1933 Mickey Mouse wearing yellow gloves and the words INGERSOLL appear on the watch face

- In 1934 "Made in the USA" was added

- In 1938 "c W.D. Ent." was added

Above: The watch in the center box is an example of the 1940s-style Mickey Mouse, while the watches that surround it are all time pieces from the 1930s, featuring a pie-eyed Mickey Mouse.

Above: A close view of a 1930s watch shows the depiction of an earlier Mickey Mouse. **Right:** By the 1940s, Mickey looked much more like the character we know today.

Collector Alert

Look for watches complete with cardboard cases. A pocket watch should have a watch fob along with the timepiece. The value is in the overall condition of the piece. Most watches were over-wound, or are non-functioning today, but this should not affect the overall value of the piece. Look for repairs or repainting on the boxes of the early watches.

Above left and left: In the 1930s, Ingersoll made these children's alarm clocks featuring Mickey Mouse. **Above:** This Mickey Mouse alarm clock dates from the 1940s.

E. R. Ives & Company
Bridgeport, Connecticut
1868 - 1932

Identification Clues

- Early toys were not marked, but have clock-work mechanisms
- Wooden toys have a folk-art appearance
- Toys are simple and mechanical; the early toys combine wood and metal
- Later toy trains are usually marked

Top: The Ives locomotive and tender was a favorite from the company's line. **Above:** A December 1914 *Good Housekeeping* magazine advertisement used the company's slogan: "Ives Toys Make Happy Boys" featured. **Right:** This cast-iron horse-drawn fire pumper with the original figure dates from the turn of the century.

In 1868 Edward Riley Ives founded his legendary company in Plymouth, Connecticut. He started out manufacturing baskets and hot-air novelty toys, which were designed to be fastened to the stove or heating vents. They jumped into action and continued with the constant surge of hot air. Ives worked on several of his designs at the Blakeslee Carriage Shop in Plymouth, owned by his brother-in-law, Cornelius Blakeslee. They worked well and joined together in a partnership of Ives & Blakeslee in 1872, changing the name to Ives, Blakeslee & Co. in 1873. The company's growth motivated the team to relocate the business to Bridgeport.

As luck would have it, Bridgeport developed into a major manufacturing city in the 1880s, and Ives took full advantage of the prime location. He utilized all the resources, including the talented designers, in the region. The toys designed by Secor, Williams and other inventors in the Bridgeport area gained popularity for their original designs and fine construction. These designs combined a clockwork mechanism with wood or tinplate, to create a variety of toys with attention-grabbing actions.

Ives' son, Harry, grew up helping his father with the business, and after his father's death in 1895 Harry C. Ives took control of the company. By this time the company was renamed the Ives Corporation. Harry helped to build the company into one of the most prestigious and respected toy manufacturers in America. He was also very active in the creation and support of the Toy Manufacturers of America (TMA).

As the country was struggling with the economic devastation of the stock market crash of 1929 and the ensuing Depression, Harry tried to save the company. Despite his continuous efforts, the company filed for bankruptcy in 1929 and was dissolved by 1932.

Top: Patented in 1876, the "Jubilee" Platform Waltzers features jointed wood and cloth dressed dancers on a pedestal on top of a dovetailed base that houses a clockwork mechanism. It is shown with its original box. **Above (1):** A tinplate locomotive and tender floor toy circa 1890s features stenciling on the engine "United States". A large bell is mounted between the locomotive and tender, which houses the bell ringer, while the flywheel is located in the undercarriage of the toy. **Above (2):** This extremely rare Ives clockwork Parlor Oarsman, patented February 9, 1869, is a hand-painted tin boat with dressed oarsman. This floor toy runs on wheels as the sailor goes through his rowing motions.

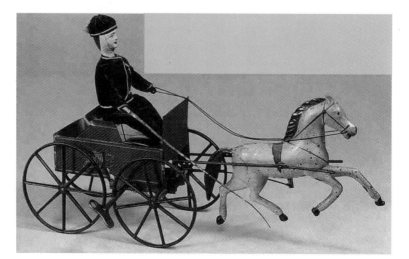

Top: Ives later made electric locomotives with passenger cars. **Above:** The electric trains were featured in a 1927 advertisement. **Above right:** This clockwork mechanism wind-up washerwoman is circa 1890s. **Right:** This extremely rare, circa-1870s clockwork mechanical horse and buggy with whipping driver features an early hand painted tin wagon with seated boy made of wood wearing a cloth suit.

Top: This Ives set featuring locomotive, tender and passenger cars is shown with its original boxes. **Above left (1):** This cast-iron bell toy entertained children by making a ringing sound when the toy was pulled across the floor. **Above left (2):** Ives' electric coal mining locomotive and three cars was a departure from the traditional locomotive sets being produced by other companies. **Far left:** The "Time Lock Savings Bank" is a still bank that helped teach two lessons: telling time and saving money. **Left:** This early Ives toy features a pair of dancers that could be activated by winding the clockwork mechanism housed within the wooden box on top of which they dance. The circa-1890s piece is shown with original box. **Above:** The Saturday Evening Post advertised the Ives toys in this 1911 advertisement.

Jumeau
Montreuil, France
1842 - 1899

Identification Clues

- Exact identification of early Jumeau dolls can be difficult because these were often not marked. If you study the markings on later dolls, they are a great help in identification.

- Dolls are incised on the back portion of the doll's neck

- Bodies are often stamped or may have paper stickers

JUMEAU

~ or ~

E. J.

~ or ~

DÉPOSÉ
JUMEAU

This French doll manufacturer attained a level of craftsmanship, materials and artistry that established it as the leader in the industry. Pierre Francois Jumeau entered into a partnership with Belton and began manufacturing fashion-type dolls on kid or wood bodies. The partnership dissolved with Belton's death, upon which Jumeau moved the factory to Montreuil, in 1873, and began to make the dolls' heads of bisque; soon after, his son Emile took over the business. Emile began to make the popular Bébés Jumeau. Both the Bébé dolls and the fashion-type dolls had pressed-bisque heads, while the later dolls (post 1890) had poured-bisque heads.

The great artistry and craftsmanship of the Jumeau dolls is generally attributed to Emile's determination to attain the highest levels of dollmaking. The dolls, with their glass paperweight eyes and highly detailed clothing, were sought-after not only in France, but internationally as well. There is a wide variety of markings on the different dolls from different eras, often the clothes are marked as well. The variety of doll models made by Jumeau included: E. J. Bébés, Tête Jumeau Bébés, Déposé Jumeau and the so-called Long-Face Jumeau.

By the turn of the twentieth century, competition from German doll manufacturers forced the French doll makers to take action and unite. In 1899, the Société Française de

Above: Jumeau was a key player during what is considered "the golden era of dollmaking" of the late nineteenth century. These bisque-headed Bébés with composition hands from the late 1890s are typical examples of the French firm's work.

Fabrication des Bébés et Jouets or SFBJ was established, with Jumeau being a founding member. The creation of the Société helped the French doll makers manufacture dolls in a larger quantity, however the quality suffered tremendously. Even after joining the SFBJ, Jumeau continued to make dolls, primarily of bisque, until 1958.

Above: This pair of fine Jumeaux, circa late 1890s, further illustrates the high level of quality found in the dolls' bisque modeling, paperweight eyes and highly detailed clothing.

Collector Alert

Excellent reproductions of antique porcelain dolls, including Jumeaux, have been made by doll artists over the past few decades. These are usually appropriately marked, so be sure to check the markings on the back of the neck or on the back. As with most French and German porcelain dolls, the marking system is complex and must be studied. Collectors who do familiarize themselves with the markings can often learn a great doll about the doll in question from its marks. Many excellent reference books have been published about this area of collecting.

Kämmer & Reinhardt
Waltershausen, Germany
1886 - 1930

Identification Clues
- Incised on the back of the head. One common system of marking is the following:

K ✡ R

SIMON & HALBIG

Above and above right: Kämmer & Reinhardt became known for the character dolls such as the wigged bisque-headed child, above right, and the bisque-headed girl, above, with her side-glancing eyes. Her short sleeves reveal her ball-jointed elbow.

Beginning in 1886, Ernst Kämmer & Franz Reinhardt produced popular designs of bisque-headed dolls with composition bodies that were quite affordable and popular around the world. Kämmer served as the designer and modeler and Reinhardt handled the business affairs. The pair created children and babies; though eventually the company became known for its character dolls, which bore more realistic expressions than the romantic French bisque dolls of the era. After Kämmer's death in 1901, the modeling was taken over by Karl Krausser, who had worked under him. The company designed the doll heads, but did not actually produce them. Most of their bisque heads were made by Simon & Halbig. They also produced some dolls with celluloid, rubber or cloth heads.

In 1902 Kämmer & Reinhardt bought the Heinrich Handwerck factory. Also beginning in this year, the Kämmer & Reinhardt dolls were produced primarily by Simon & Halbig, using the Kämmer & Reinhardt molds. The company claimed to be the first to include teeth in bisque doll heads. In 1909, the introduction of character dolls on bent-limb baby bodies was a newsworthy event. In 1920 Kämmer & Reinhardt acquired the Simon & Halbig factory.

Kenton Hardware Company
Kenton, Ohio
1890 - 1953

The Kenton Lock Manufacturing Company began by producing refrigerator hardware that F. M. Perkins of Cleveland, Ohio, had patented. Four years later the first line of cast-iron toys was manufactured.

The company first introduced a cast-iron, single-horse-drawn road cart. This opened the door for producing cast-iron mechanical banks, stoves and more elaborate horse-drawn fire wagons. Toy production grew to become a major part of the company's production and in 1900, the name was changed to the Kenton Hardware Manufacturing Company.

In 1903 tragedy struck when the Kenton factory burned to the ground. The company quickly responded by rebuilding a new and improved factory with increased manufacturing capabilities. As the country entered the era of motorized vehicles, Kenton recognized an opportunity to become a pioneer in manufacturing automotive toys. Altering the toy designs from cast-iron carriages to cast-iron automotive toys was a risk that proved to

be quite successful and earned the company recognition as the largest manufacturer of automotive toys in the United States.

The cast-iron mechanical banks also became quite popular. During the next ten years the company experienced managerial and financial turbulence. By 1915, the company was renamed the Kenton Hardware Company, and Louis S. Bixler was named president and general manager. Prior to joining Kenton, Bixler had worked for Hubley where he had gained firsthand experience in toy manufacturing. Bixler brought this experience to help toy production at Kenton soar. The aim of production focused on cars and trucks. From 1920 through 1935, sales from the automotive line reached record highs, and the pieces continued to be popular through the early 1950s. Due to financial troubles, the company ceased production in 1952 and the company assets, including toy molds and designs, were sold in 1953.

Identification Clues

- Horse-drawn toys like fire toys, carriages, drays, and "Overland Circus"
- Removable figures on the carriages, drays, fire toys and horse-drawn toys
- Logo "The Real Thing in Everything but Size"

Top: This over-sized fire pumper is 27 inches in overall length. It is cast iron and has an open-slat wagon with large boiler. **Above:** The box label for a dump wagon #211 features the Kenton logo. **Left:** Among Kenton's wide variety of cast-iron toys was this oxen-pulled cart with driver.

The Kenton toys on this page illustrate the progression in design from the early 1900s, shown in the top photos, through to the 1950s, shown in the bottom photos. Notice the changes in paint, use of cast iron and the look of the horses through the decades.

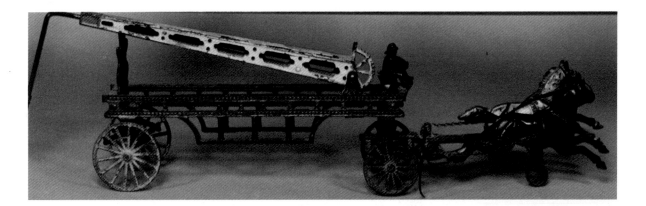

The toys on this page represent the diversity of items produced by Kenton, and the type of toys that are typically found today at flea markets or garage sales.

Kestner & Co.
Waltershausen, Germany
1805 - 1938

One of the oldest doll manufacturers in the world, this company was founded by Johannes Daniel Kestner in 1805. He first made papier-mâché notebooks and wooden shirt buttons. By 1820 he was making wooden and papier-mâché dolls as well. After his death in 1858, his grandson, Adolf Kestner, experimented with papier-mâché headed dolls on leather or cloth bodies in the 1860s. By the 1870s, Kestner had begun making bisque-headed dolls on cloth, wood, kid-leather and, later, composition, bodies, to keep up with competition in his country as well as in France. He eventually bought a porcelain factory in Ohrdruf, at which he made bisque heads for other German companies, as well. Kestner is said to have been one of the first firms to make dressed dolls, and was one of the few to make dolls in their entirety at their own factory. Kestner dolls were primarily baby and child dolls; some had celluloid heads that were made for Kestner by other companies from Kestner's molds. Kestner dolls bear a variety of markings; after 1892, they were marked "Made in Germany" with a mold number.

Above: These four dolls feature bisque heads and open mouths, and originate from the early 1900s. The examples on the far left and third from left are shoulder heads on kid leather bodies, while the other two dolls have composition bodies.

Collector Alert

Check bisque for hairline cracks or peppering (black flecks) from the firing process. This will decrease the value of the doll. Excellent reproductions of antique porcelain dolls, including Kestners, have been made by doll artists over the past few decades. These are usually appropriately marked, so be sure to check the markings on the back of the neck or on the back. As with most French and German porcelain dolls, Kestner's marking system is complex and must be studied. Collectors who do familiarize themselves with the markings can often learn a great doll about the doll in question from its marks. Many excellent reference books have been published about this area of collecting.

Above left: This open-mouth bisque-headed doll on a composition body bears an example of the Kestner logo on the front of her dress. **Far left:** This pair of Kestner bisque-headed dolls illustrates the variety of sizes available from the company. **Left:** This shoulder-head doll with bisque arms on a kid body dates from the early 1900s.

Keystone Manufacturing Company
Boston, Massachusetts
1925 - 1957

By the second decade of the twentieth century, toy manufacturers were recognizing that social trends recreated in miniature opened up a wide new consumer market. Keystone was one of the makers aware of this phenomenon, and took special note that motion pictures were taking the country by storm. The popularity of this new entertainment medium provided Keystone with their first toy line.

Keystone grew out of the partnership formed by Ben and Isidore Marks, who had created the Marks Brothers Company in 1911 to supply human-hair doll wigs and celluloid doll heads to American doll manufacturers. The company went on to produce rag dolls, jack-in-the-boxes, celluloid pin wheels, tin horns and mechanical voice boxes for dolls. At the 1919 New York Toy Fair, the brothers introduced their moving picture machine, which was greeted with great success. In 1924 they bought the American Pictograph Company of Manchester, New Hampshire and the combined companies became Keystone.

As Keystone, the company first produced motion picture toys featuring Charlie Chaplin and Tom Mix films. The Keystone Movie graph machines were a big hit, allowing children to enjoy the "movies" at home. After this early success, Keystone began to expand their manufacturing line to include the ever-popular automotive line.

The American economy was prospering and Keystone noticed the increase in the number of toy autos being produced by a variety of competitors. Realizing that the company needed to establish itself with a product that separated their trucks from other manufacturers, Keystone approached the Packard Motor Company for permission to recreate and market trucks modeled after the popular Packard design. The request was granted and the Keystone Packard truck, featuring the popular radiator and logo, made its debut in 1925. The trucks also featured a 22-gauge cold rolled steel body, nickel hub caps and radiator cap, a see-through celluloid windshield, front cranks, headlamps, signal arms for 'stop' and 'go', steering capabilities, and for fifty cents extra, rubber tires.

The Keystone Packard truck was a huge success, and became a serious rival of the current market leader, Buddy L. In the fight for market dominance, Keystone advertising stressed all the special features that distin-

---

Top: This Keystone water pump tower pressed-steel truck features a real pump that worked on a hand lever action. **Left:** Keystone promoted its toys in magazine advertisements like this one from 1949.

guished their toy Packard truck from all the other toy trucks on the market. One ad campaign even guaranteed that a two-hundred-pound man could stand on the toy without damage. Their efforts paid off with a growth in sales and a strong market share.

This popularity helped Keystone weather the era of the Depression. Manufacturing slowed but did not hinder the creative powers of the design staff. Still striving to stand out in the market, Keystone released a Siren Riding Toy in 1934, which had a saddle seat in the bed of the toy and handlebars in front for steering. The overwhelming positive response of the public pushed the designers to create a new sturdy and affordable riding toy. Two years later Keystone released a new creation, the Ride-Em mail plane. The toy measured 25 inches long, was constructed sturdy enough for a small child to ride and was affordably priced at two dollars.

Top: This Keystone pump engine has ladders and brass railings. Under the hood is a high-pressure pump that is activated by a front hand crank and a hand-operated siren. **Above:** This water pump tower truck features a removable child seat, hand siren and a hand lever with real pump action. **Above left:** This Keystone Ride 'Em plane with a child's seat and handle bars on fuselage with revolving propeller has the rust and play-wear that is typical on these large pressed-steel toys.

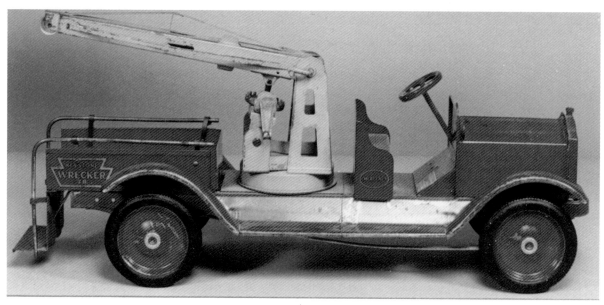

Top: This pressed-steel Ride 'Em dump truck has a handle and seat. **Above:** The wrecker features an open cab and revolving hoist crane. **Right:** This Ride 'Em dump truck has a wooden handle and missing seat.

Kiddie-Kar (The H.C. White Co.,)

Bennington, Vermont
1915 - 1930s

The patent for this toy was registered in 1879; however, production of the Kiddie-Kar did not hit the consumer market till 1915. The H. C. White Company of Bennington, Vermont, had developed a simple concept of a bicycle that a small child could maneuver easily and safely. The wooden Kiddie-Kar consisted of a single front wheel attached to a steering wheel and two back wheels and a seat. (Fifty years later, a similar description could have applied to Marx's Big Wheel.)

The Kiddie-Kar was quite popular with children and parents alike. It was a transition toy to help muscles develop before the child graduated on to a bicycle. The toy was well-built and sturdy, however many Kiddie-Kars were left outside to battle the elements, or discarded after the owner outgrew it, so not many have survived.

Today, the term "Kiddie-Kar" is used for any small vehicle that children drive, that is powered by pedals or foot motions, such as the pressed-steel pedal cars manufactured by Steelcraft or Metalcraft in the 1940s and 1950s. However, the term was originally developed by the H.C. White Company for its particular toy.

Identification Clues

- Look for company label on toy
- Large front wheel, seat and pair of smaller, same-sized back wheels

Above left: This photograph of a young boy on his Kiddie-Kar illustrates the easy and safe maneuvering of the toy. **Above:** This lively advertisement for the wooden Kiddie-Kar dates from 1920.

Kilgore Manufacturing Company
Westerville, Ohio
1925 - 1978

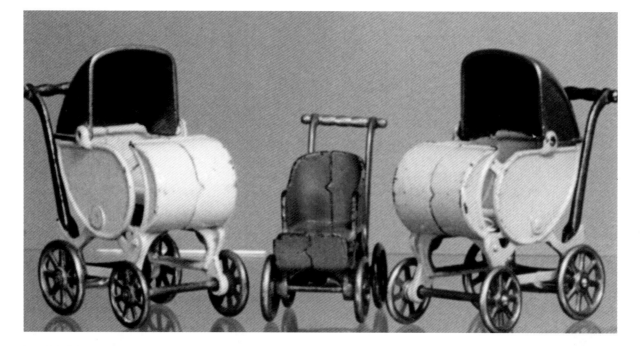

"Toys that last" was the motto of this company that produced cast-iron toy cap guns and cannons. The phrase pushed the company to develop and manufacture toys in support of this statement.

In 1925, Kilgore decided to take over the Dayton, Ohio-based George D. Wanner Company. The largest producer of kites in America, Wanner made a E-Z FLY tail-less kite that was a welcome addition to Kilgore's production line. In addition to kites and cap guns, the company followed the lead of other toy manufacturers by adding automotive toys to their line. Since the cap guns were made of cast iron, the addition of fire engines, cars and trucks made of cast iron was a natural addition to the manufacturing line. With all the materials available, the company was able to mass-produce the new line with very little additional expense.

The toys were produced in boxed sets that sold for fifty cents, and were distributed around the country by Butler Brothers, the largest wholesale jobber in America. They became Kilgore's largest account. By 1929, the company was doing quite well with their focused area of toy production. Kilgore weathered the Depression by redirecting production to consist only of the cast-iron cap guns and paper caps. In 1937 Kilgore became one of the first toy companies to begin producing plastic toys. This change helped the company stay in business producing its original product line in plastic through 1978.

Top: Kilgore's cast-iron baby carriage, center, has spoked wheels, while the other two carriages have nickel hood covers. **Right:** The Kilgore two-seat convertible has nickel accents and nickel disc wheels.

Kingsbury Manufacturing Company
Keene, New Hampshire
1919 - 1942

H arry Thayer Kingsbury founded this company with the blessing of his grandfather and the financing that went with it, which allowed Kingsbury to purchase the Wilkins Toy Company around 1895. He also spotted an opportunity when the Clipper Machine Works was partially destroyed by fire, quickly buying the company and combining it with his earlier acquisition.

Kingsbury continued to produce toys under the Wilkins name and was beginning to make a name for himself within the industry. Following the lead of other toy manufacturers of the time, his company jumped on the automotive toy bandwagon. In 1910, the company released its first production of automobiles, which continued to dominate the company's production up to World War I. The plant completely converted to manufacturing war supplies to support the American initiative overseas. Once the war was over, the company resumed production with materials and designs used before the war, making only mod-

erate changes, until manufacturing was back to full speed and an updated line could be created. The new designs were based on actual cars and airplanes of the time. It was 1919 and these miniature versions stimulated children's imaginations to pretend they were being transported around the yard in a fast car or taking a ride around the living room in an airplane. These new designs were continually updated to mirror the constant changing designs in the real world. During this rebuilding period Kingsbury decided to drop the Wilkins name and to rename his company as the Kingsbury Manufacturing Company.

In 1920 Kingsbury's sons, Edward and Chester, joined the company. They added the Kingsbury Machine Tool Division, which grew rapidly. By the 1940s the new division had received a number of war contracts, which began to dominate overall production. Kingsbury decided to sell the toy division to Keystone in Boston; the tool division continued to produce tools for various companies.

Above: This Kingsbury fire pumper of sheet metal with rubber tires, disc wheels and clockwork mechanism is shown with a Kingsbury ladder truck in pressed steel with rubber tires, metal wheels and clockwork mechanism.

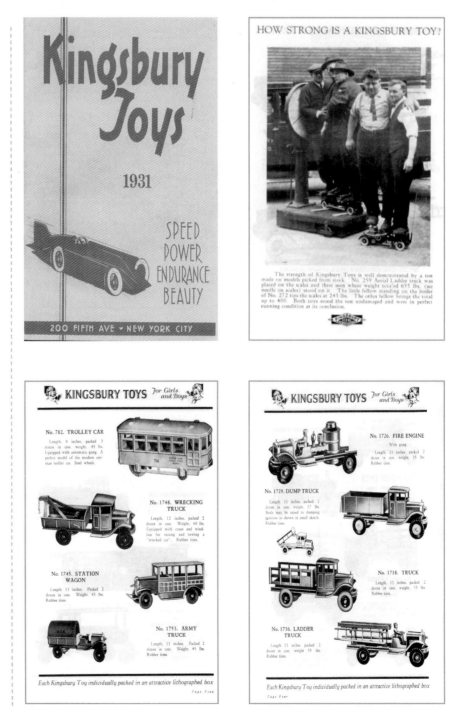

Top: Among Kingsbury's earliest cast-iron pieces were fire toys, like this example. **Above right and right:** The cover and inside pages of Kingsbury's 1931 catalog promote the strength and endurance of the toys.

Knickerbocker Toy Company
New York, New York
1920s - 1960s

The Knickerbocker story begins more than one hundred years ago with a family of Dutch immigrants, the Van Whyes, who came to America in the mid-1800s and settled in Albany, New York. At this time the predominately English and French population of New York State used the word Knickerbocker to refer to the early Dutch setters who populated regions throughout the state. The Van Whye family established their toy manufacturing company around 1850 and chose to legally and permanently change their family name to Knickerbocker, as well as to utilize the name for their new company.

The young company produced lithographed-paper-on-wood alphabet blocks in addition to a variety of wooden puzzles and educational toys. By 1922, the Knickerbocker Toy Company had moved to New York City and began expanding the line of toys to include stuffed dolls, animals and marionettes. During the mid-1920s the company also began manufacturing stuffed bears, which were made of mohair and jointed, with noses of felt, embroidery or metal.

By the late 1920s, Walt Disney and his staff were busy developing and perfecting a new form of entertainment, animated short films. Disney's first venture was *Steamboat Willie*, featuring Mickey Mouse. By this time, Mickey was a popular comic strip character in newspapers across the country. With the production of *Steamboat Willie*, in which Walt Disney himself provided the character's voice, audiences could see and hear Mickey. By the mid 1930s, Mickey, Minnie Mouse, and Donald Duck were household names for children across the country. The Knickerbocker Com-

Identification Clues

- Features of Knickerbocker bears and soft toys include:

1920 – 1930s
- Metal or black-stitched nose
- Pointed muzzle
- Glass or tin eyes
- Large cupped ears set wide apart on a round head
- Oval feet
- Velveteen or felt pads
- Fully jointed

1940s
- Long mohair,
- Inset muzzle of short mohair or velveteen
- Glass eyes
- "Animals of Distinction" tag
- Fully jointed

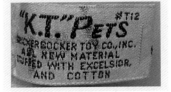

Above: Household names by the mid 1930s, the characters of Mickey and Minnie Mouse were reproduced as cloth dolls by Knickerbocker. These examples from the 1930s have composition shoes and their original paper tags.

Above left: Another popular character in the 1930s was Disney's Donald Duck. Knickerbocker made this long-billed cloth example in the late 1930s. **Above right:** The Cowboy Mickey Mouse cloth doll is complete with hat, lasso, chaps, guns and composition shoes.

pany, which was by now established as a major American manufacturer, recognized the popularity of Disney's characters and approached him with the concept of reproducing his creations in composition, cloth and plush. The company was granted licenses from Disney, and the popular characters, along with teddy bears, dominated the production line during this period. The simple design of these toys captured the magic of Mickey and Minnie and made the stuffed toys quite popular.

During the 1930s the company produced a bear called Winston the good-luck bear or, as he is also known, the fertility bear. The story goes that a mother presented the bear to her daughter who was having trouble conceiving a child. The mother instructed her daughter to keep the bear on the bed and the bear would bring her luck. Within a year the daughter happily gave birth to her first child. The Knickerbocker Toy Company does not guarantee similar results but the folklore of the story and the nostalgia of the bear make him more appealing.

From the 1930s through the 1960s, the company expanded into manufacturing a variety of licensed toys and collectibles, which included: Raggedy Ann & Andy; Holly Hobbie; Nancy and Sluggo; Hanna-Barbera characters; and Smokey the Bear, just to name a few. The Knickerbocker teddy bear business was also very

strong during this time period and the company came up with several slogans that appeared on the label with the company's logo. "Animals of Distinction" was in use during the 1940s and the company adopted the motto "Joy of a Toy" in the 1950s. These slogans appeared on packaging and boxes for the toys, dolls and bears. After years of many business changes, including discontinuation of toy production for much of the 1980s, the revitalized company continues to produce dolls and collectibles today.

Knickerbocker bears made in the 1920s and 1930s have been increasing in value, as more and more collectors have grown interested in collecting

bears and soft toys. This is due in part to the rich history the company possesses as well as the craftsmanship that went into the production of the teddy bears and other toys produced during most of this century. Collectors around the world agree that if a bear is not marked, it can be difficult to positively identify the manufacturer, country of origin or date produced. We do know Knickerbocker bears were mass-produced from 1920 through 1960 and that Smokey the bear was about the only bear manufactured during the 1970s. The identification clues include a few pointers that may help identify your bruin as a Knickerbocker.

Collector Alert

Because children loved to play with these toys, it is difficult to find them in good condition today. Look for pieces that are complete with all the accessories, in good condition and if possible, the paper tags. These are truly some of the finest examples of early Disney characters around.

Above: Knickerbocker continued to make Disney characters in the 1940s, such as these Pinocchio and Jiminy Cricket composition dolls from that decade, which are complete down to their often-missing hats.

Top: This fully jointed mohair Knickerbocker bear, left, has a metal nose. The legendary fully jointed mohair Winston Bear, right, has glass eyes and is stuffed with excelsior. **Above left:** This circa 1920s fully jointed black Knickerbocker mohair bear has a stitched nose and velveteen pads. **Above:** This small mohair bear has the company label sewn into the middle of the bear's stomach. **Above right:** This plush bear's muzzle is a contrasting color; the bear has a company tag in its side seam.

Käthe Kruse Doll Company
Donauwörth, Germany
1910

For the past ninety years, the Käthe Kruse Doll Company has been a major part of the international doll world. Käthe Kruse's doll-making career spanned nearly five decades, from 1911 to 1956. She never dreamed of international manufacturing success, but instead focused her company philosophy on what a doll should mean to a child. "A child for a child, cozy and warm," she maintained. "The secret of the doll lies in its childlike, natural expression, and a doll should appeal to one's feelings." All of these ideas influenced Käthe Kruse in her design choices and how she ran her company.

Käthe Kruse was born Katharina Simon on September 17, 1883, in Breslau, Germany. At an early age, she expressed an interest in poetry, nature, and theatre and studied acting as a teenager. At the age of seventeen, she ventured to Berlin where she landed a job with a theatre company and took to the stage with the name Hedda Somin. Her career blossomed as she continued to work in Berlin as well as to tour Europe, including Warsaw and Moscow.

In the first half of the twentieth century, Berlin was a mecca for artists and performers. Attitudes and values were more relaxed than in any other city in Europe and this exposure to a more open way of thinking about art, life and relationships shaped the young woman's thinking.

When she was nineteen, she met Max Kruse, a forty-seven-year-old sculptor who lived in Berlin. They viewed life and love in a very similar fashion. Hedda decided to give up the stage, take back her name of Katharina and venture into a relationship with Max. She was a modern woman who knew she wanted a relationship and children, but believed strongly that marriage was not in the picture for her at this time.

Identification Clues

- Käthe Kruse signature stamped with number on left foot
- Paper tag with recreated signature (very rare)
- Dolls had painted hair through the 1920s; after that decade wigs were used as well
- Doll produced by Kämmer & Reinhardt in 1911 has ball-jointed body and turning head

Above: This 1914 photo of Käthe Kruse's and her family includes her husband, Max Kruse, and five of their children: Fifi, Michel, Jochen, Hannerle and Mimmerle.

Top: In 1925 Käthe Kruse posed with her examples of her Du Mein Doll I and Doll II. Above: This romantic windblown photo of the doll known as Ilsebill was taken in 1938.

They had two girls within two years and, in 1904, relocated to the countryside of Switzerland. As their eldest daughter, Mimerle, grew older she constantly asked for a doll that was like her little sister Fifi, a baby soft and warm. Katharina asked her husband to shop around Berlin to find dolls for her young daughters. He wrote back: "I won't buy any dolls here in Berlin. They are all ugly, stiff and cold. How can a child play and grow proper mothering instincts with such hard, cold and stiff things? Start to make your own, this will allow you to develop your artistic feelings and skills." Katharina took the challenge and created Oskar—a doll with a potato head and sand-filled body for a more realistic look and feel. This was the seed of the doll company that still exists today. Katharina perfected her designs over the next five years and continued to stress the durability of her designs and well as the realistic look of the dolls.

By 1909, Katharina and Max had

eight children and decided it was time they married. Katharina took Max's last name, Kruse. In 1910 she was invited to display her designs in the "Homemade Toys" show sponsored at the Herman Tietz Department Store in Berlin. The dolls created by Kruse, which had a classic child's head, handpainted, on a cloth body filled with wood shavings, received tremendous praise and publicity. Doll manufacturers were impressed with her vision and looked to her for inspiration. Kämmer & Reinhardt, well known throughout the world for their mass-production of bisque dolls, offered her a contract to produce and distribute her creations. The result was disappointing to Kruse. The industrial production of her designs lacked the personal touch she was striving for in the creation of dolls and did not meet her artistic standards, so she terminated the contract and bought back the rights to her original designs after only a couple months of production. Her own

commercially produced dolls, girls and boys known as Doll I, created between 1911 and 1933, have round bodies stuffed with nettle cloth, sewn-on arms and jointed legs. The thumbs are separated and the fingers are individually seamed. The heads are hand-molded nettle cloth, with molded face masks, stuffed with wood shavings and painted by hand. (Later dolls have machine-molded nettle-cloth heads and sewn-on thumbs.)

Positive word-of-mouth publicity about the dolls featured at the Tietz show, however, had traveled the world. Shortly after her separation from Kämmer & Reinhardt, Kruse received an order from F.A.O. Schwarz in America for one hundred and fifty dolls. Determined to meet the challenge and fill the order, she hired a small staff and enlisted the assistance of her husband to help meet the deadline and send the dolls off to America. The reception in America for the dolls was so great that another order for five hundred more was placed, and Kruse established her own manufacturing company to meet the demands of a growing global response to her creations.

Käthe Kruse continued to run her company through changing times and world events. By 1953, at the age of seventy, she turned the running of the company over to her son Max, daughter Hanne and Hanne's husband, Heinz Alder. She died on July 19, 1968, just prior to her eighty-fifth birthday. But the dolls, under the direction of Andrea and Steve Christenson in Donauwörth, continue to be made and appreciated today.

Top left: This doll was known as *Rotkappchen*, or little Red Riding Hood. **Top right:** Jockerle and Margretchen date from 1913. **Above:** The doll known as Mareile Doll I also dates from 1913.

Kyser & Rex
Philadelphia, Pennsylvania
1880 - 1884

Identification Clues

We know the company produced the following banks:

- Butting Buffalo Bank
- Chimpanzee Bank
- Confectionary Bank
- Globe Savings Bank
- Motor Bank
- Organ Bank Boy and Girl
- Organ Bank Monkey
- Organ Bank Cat and Dog
- Organ Grinder and Performing Bear
- Roller Skating Bank

Collector Alert

As on all cast-iron toys, check the casting to ensure the surface is smooth. Grainy surfaces indicate a reproduction. Also be cautious of repainting or restorations.

L. Kyser and Alfred Rex founded this cast-iron mechanical bank manufacturing company. Although the company was only in business for a very short time, it produced some of the banks most sought-after by collectors today. The short production period makes it possible to individually identify many of the banks made by Kyser & Rex.

Top left: To operate The Mikado cast-iron mechanical bank, circa 1886, a penny is placed under the hat in the Mikado's right hand. Upon the turning of the lever the coin disappears, then reappears under the hat in his left hand while bells chime. **Top right:** To operate The Lion and Monkey cast-iron mechanical bank, patented July 17, 1883, a penny is placed in the monkey's hand. When the lever is pushed, the coin falls into the open lion's mouth. **Above:** The Boy Stealing Watermelon cast-iron mechanical bank is circa 1894. A coin is put in a slot; and the lever is pressed. When coin disappears, the dog runs out to attack the boy, whose hand is withdrawn from the melon.

Lehmann
Brandenberg, Germany
1881

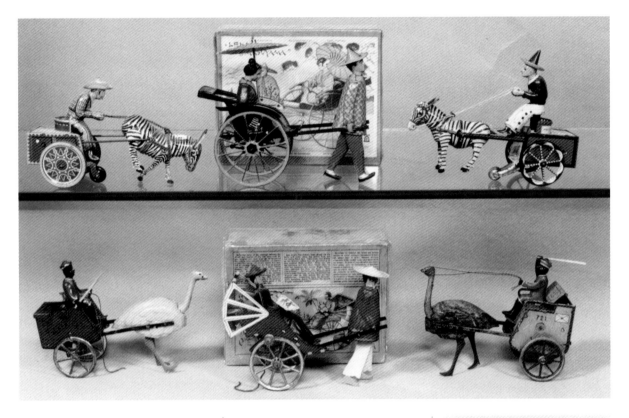

inplate containers were this company's main product when it began manufacturing in 1881. Originally located in Brandenburg, Germany, the company was reestablished in Nuremberg in 1951, where it still remains. Lehmann soon grew highly experienced in producing tinplate with highly colorful lithography, which allowed it to tap into the toy market—slowly at first, then with full force. The early toys were figures like dancers and boys on bicycles; by 1914 Lehmann, like other toy companies around the world, moved into the production of toy vehicles.

In response to heavy competition in the marketplace, Lehmann developed imaginative mechanisms in their toys that helped the vehicles stand out. One unique concept was the use of the friction wheel and coil springs to provide animation. The inventory expanded to include buses, cars, and a variety of animals pulling carts, cabs and movable figures. Close to ninety percent of the company's production was exported to countries around the world. The toys were clearly marked and thus could be easily identified.

The vast quantities of Lehmann toys exported around the world found their way to the shores of the United States, and from 1895 until World War II, toys poured into the country. As the war approached, production slowed, and after the war, severe restrictions were placed on toy production. In 1948 Lehmann was taken over by VEB Mechanische Spielwaren.

Identification Clues

- Examine the piece for the logo shown below, which is usually easy to find
- The mark in the center of the bell stands for the initials of the company founder, Ernst Paul Lehmann. This mark sometimes appears alone on a toy.

MARKE

LEHMANN

Above: Lehmann's use of exotic animals for a variety of toy designs is showcased in this grouping featuring zebras and ostriches. **Right:** This extermely rare toy is known as the Boxer. A small figure is thrown about by four other Chinese figures. The toy was based upon the "Boxer" secret society that existed during the occupation of China in the early 1900s.

Collector Alert

Look out for repaired or replaced wind-up mechanisms. Replaced parts or re-painting will decrease the value of the toy.

Top: A pair of Wild West Bucking Bronco lithographed-tin wind-up toys are shown here in two versions, with an original box. In the second row are the duck and duckling lithographed wind-up known as PAAK-PAK. **Above:** The Miss Blondin lithographed-tin rope dancer was named afer the famous tightrope walker. The toy is shown with its original box. **Above right:** Lithographed-tinplate dirigibles and zeppelins were among the wide variety of wind-up toys created by Lehmann. **Right:** A pair of Balky Mule toys makes use of a comical clown and donkey for its subject. The Zikra-Dare-Devil toy, featuring a kicking zebra, is shown with its original box. A cowboy rider is pulled by a zebra in the 1954 Gallop toy, which displays the new color scheme the company used in later years.

Top: Lehmann's vehicles were very popular offerings, and a great variety was produced to satisfy the demand. Above: The company often gave its toys memorable names. The toy at the far left in the row second from bottom is called Naughty Boy; in the same row there is an AHA delivery van and a motor car. All three are shown with their original boxes. In the bottom row, from left, are a Buster Brown wind-up, presumably made for the U.S. market, an Auto Post lithographed-tinplate wind-up and a Mars tank.

Behind The Scenes

During an appraisal day in Portland, Oregon, a young woman and her mother approached and placed a small box before me. The box appeared to be in very good condition and the lithographed tinplate Lehmann toy on the inside was in brand-new condition. The young woman took a wind-up swing toy out of the box and placed the small doll in the seat of the swing. In the bottom of the box was the original receipt for the purchase of the toy for $1.51 in 1898. There was also a photograph of the original owner of the toy at age seven, dated 1900. The box had no elaborate labels or markings, and since only the toy was marked with the Lehmann trademark, the family had no idea of the manufacturer of the toy or its history.

To find this type of documentation, which substantiates the year of production and confirms the family history, with photographs, is far more than one could expect at an appraisal fair. I detailed the history of the company and told the family that vintage Lehmann toys are sought after by collectors around the world. The family could not believe the family heirloom had any significant value. To them the sentimental value was more than enough. I explained that at one of Bill Bertoia's auctions several Lehmann toys, in similar condition to their lithographed wind-up toy, but without the box, had brought $4,000 each. Adding the original box, receipt and documentation could increase the estimated value of their family heirloom to range from $5,000 -$6,000.

The look on both women's faces was worth the trip to Oregon. They told me after the appraisal that they had wanted to find out the value of the toy because the third-generation daughter, who was turning four, had found the toy in a drawer, opened the box and started playing with it. Grandma discovered the little girl just as she was going to wind the toy and throw the doll across the room. They immediately told me that the little girl would no longer play with the toy. I suggested that if the toy was to remain in the family, it would be a good idea to take a photograph of grandma, mom and daughter with the toy to preserve the continuing history of its ownership.

Top: An Ajax clockwork acrobat stands next to a tinplate porter known as Adam, pushing a hand-cart. In the second row is a pair of Zigzag toys; another example of Miss Blondin; and Paddy and the Pig, shown with its original box. **Above:** The man walking the two dogs is a wind-up toy known as Sink-Sank Lehmann Family. The walking couple below him are commonly known as Walking down Broadway. Their action is started by a flywheel spinning on a cogwheel set in motion by a patented rack system. This is the only toy Lehmann produced using this system. Next to this couple is a Skirolf wind-up and Captain of Kopenivk, a figure that resembled the sham artist cobbler who stole treasury money. **Above left:** Another example of the Ajax clockwork acrobat is seen from a different angle. **Left:** This is another example of the Captain of Kopenivk toy.

Top: This trio of waltzing dolls stands on a wheeled platform. Each doll has a celluloid head and tin body and hands. The next row shows a magic ball dancer toy; a swing doll wind-up; and a Hop Hop tinplate toy. **Above:** The AHA Delivery Van is shown with its original box, as is the pair of Tut-Tut automobile toys. In the bottom row are OHO, LOLO AUTO, ALSO automobile and an Autin, featuring an American boy in a pedal car. **Above right:** The original box for the waltzing dolls showed the figures. **Right:** Another example of Adam the tinplate wind-up porter pushes his handcart.

Top: Tap-Tap the walking gardener with his wheelbarrow is shown with the original box. Next to this toy is an Express clockwork toy of a porter pulling a trunk. The next row features a Zulu ostrich mail toy; a NA-OB driver with a donkey cart; and Africa, an ostrich mail wind-up.
Above: Lehmann produced a variety of clockwork airplane toys; these are shown with original boxes.
Right: The Ikarus airplane has wire-supported paper wings and an open-frame fuselage. It is shown with its original box.

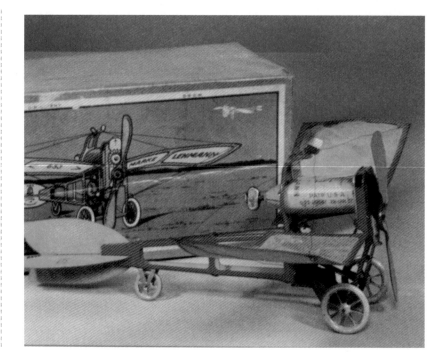

Top: Lehmann vehicles included the Autobus lithgraphed tinplate double-decker bus; the IHI Meat Van tin delivery truck, with cloth sides that open; and an Auto Post red mail van. Left: Among the company's popular toys was The Wild West Bucking Bronco. Above: The original box for the Wild West Bucking Bronco shows the toy in action.

Lenci
Turin, Italy
1919

- Side-glancing eyes
- Zigzag seam on the back of the head.
- Separately stitched outer fingers and two inner fingers joined together
- Stamped in black or purple on the foot

This Italian doll company started as a hobby for Elena Scavini, who began making dolls from felt. The dolls became quite popular in their hometown of Turin and after only five years of production were featured in the American magazine, *Playthings*. Elena's husband Enrico officially named the company Lenci in 1922; the letters represent the Latin motto *Ludus Est Nobis Constanter Industria*, which can be loosely translated to mean either: Play is our constant work or Play is work for us. The first trademark, registered in 1919, shows a child's spinning top surrounded by the words of this motto.

The Scavinis brought together many famous Italian artists and designers who created, in addition to dolls, a plethora of clothing, handbags, accessories and various home furnishing, including ceramics. The Lenci dolls were advertised as artistic display pieces, and the rich colors of the felt, the intricate hand embroidery and the felt appliques all supported this advertising. Always bearing a high-style Art Deco look, the dolls represented children; exotic figures; beautiful ladies and dancers; international celebrities; character pieces; and harlequins. The Lenci Company continues to produce felt dolls of high quality, with expressive faces and elaborate costuming today, though in a much smaller range of characters.

Top: The Lenci dolls are recognizable by their felt bodies and clothing, as well as their expressive faces. The long-limbed lady at far left wears the typical elaborate clothing of the early dolls; the child at center left is an early Lenci known as Alma, while the girl in the box is a contemporary re-issue of a 1927 Lenci doll. **Left:** Lenci made dolls in costumes of a variety of countries; this early piece represents a Dutchman.

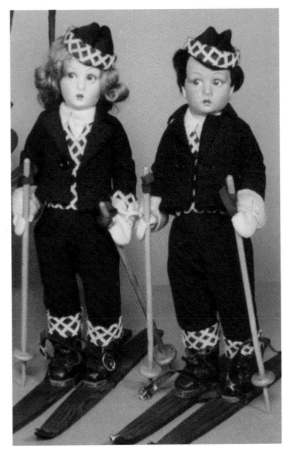

Collector Alert

The condition of the felt greatly affects the value of the dolls. The fabric can attract moths and the colors of the felt fade from contact with direct sunlight. Many Lenci-type felt dolls were also produced by a variety of firms during the 1920s-1940s. Because Lenci continues to produce dolls based upon old designs, look carefully at tags and markings.

Top, from left: This girl with her dog is shown with her original Liberty of London box; the boy wears a detailed riding outfit while the coachman, standing 17 inches high, is a tea cosy. The vivid colors of the felt Lenci used will endure through time if the dolls are properly stored. **Far left:** This pair of skiers wear matching felt jackets, pants and hats trimmed with a lattice-work felt design. **Left:** Many firms made similarly styled dolls, such as this Lenci-type lady.

Lincoln Logs
Chicago, Illinois
1920

One of America's greatest natural resources during the late 1860s was the abundance of pine trees. Joel Ellis was manufacturing toys in Vermont under three different firm names: Ellis, Britton and Eaton; Vermont Novelty Works; and the Cooperative Manufacturing Company. After the Civil War, he utilized the plentiful wood to design and manufacture small wooden logs that could be used to construct a variety of buildings, stimulating the Victorian era child's imagination. The timing of this Ellis creation was about fifty years too early—for it was John Lloyd Wright, son of the famous architect Frank Lloyd Wright, who, in 1916, used the same concept to make the popular Lincoln Logs. He patented his creation on August 31, 1920.

The conception of the building toy is a classic example of a plaything's creation being inspired by, and based upon, a "real-life" creation. John Lloyd Wright was traveling with his father to Japan where the elder Wright had been commissioned to provide a design for the Imperial Hotel in Tokyo. The challenge in the design of the building was that it must withstand the occasional earthquake that was not uncommon in this region of Japan. While construction was underway, the younger Wright took special notice of the overlapping construction used in the creation of the building's foundation to give the building the necessary flexibility during an earthquake. This construction also inspired John to create a toy that has entertained the imaginations and creativity of children around the world for more than eighty years. The toy continues to be manufactured today by Playskool, a division of Hasbro, Inc.

Above and left: Advertising for Lincoln Logs in magazines such as *Child Life* illustrated the variety of projects children could create with the building toys. The advertisements shown here appeared in April 1923, December 1927 and December 1928.

FRONT ELEVATION

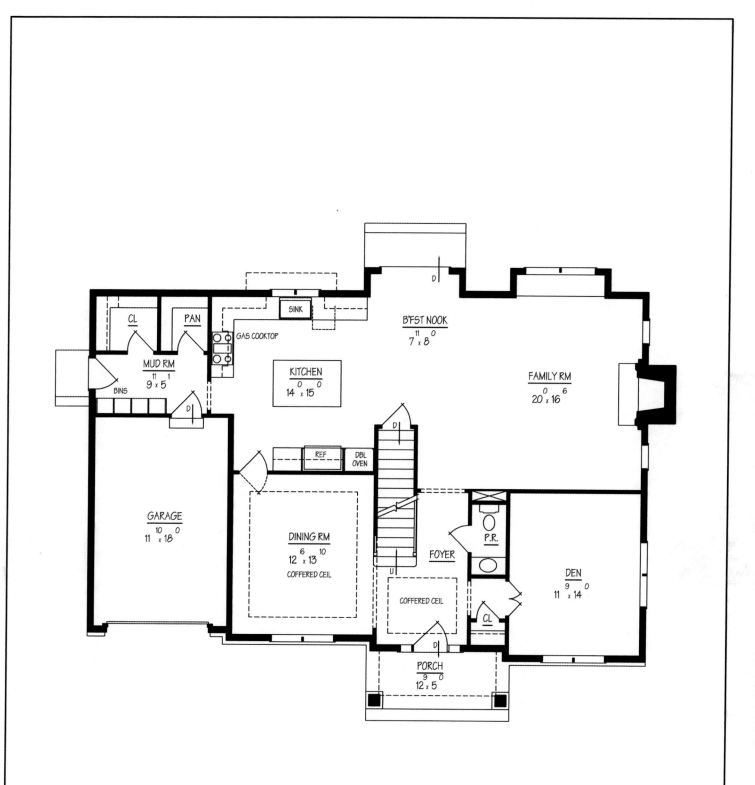

CL

PAN

SINK

GAS COOKTOP

B'FST NOOK
7 x 8

FAMILY RM
20 x 16

MUD RM
9 x 5

BINS

KITCHEN
14 x 15

REF

DBL
OVEN

D

GARAGE
11 x 18

DINING RM
12 x 13
COFFERED CEIL

P.R.

FOYER

DEN
11 x 14

COFFERED CEIL

CL

PORCH
12 x 5

FIRST FLOOR PLAN

1333 SQ. FT. MAIN
229 SQ. FT. GARAGE
63 SQ. FT. PORCH

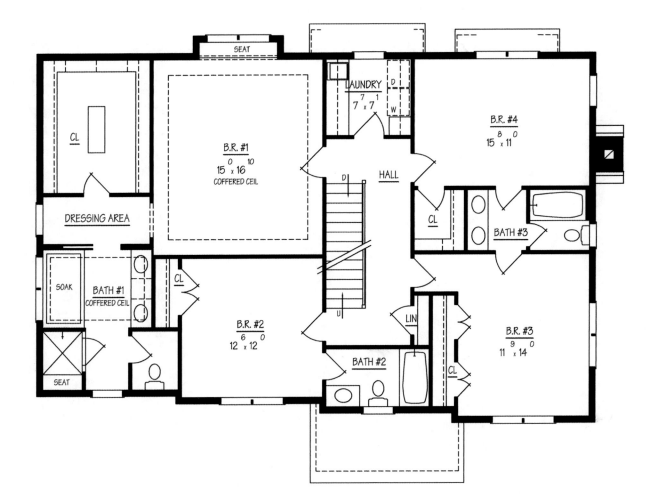

SEAT

CL

B.R. #1
0   10
15 x 16
COFFERED CEIL.

LAUNDRY
7   1
7 x 7

D
W

D

HALL

B.R. #4
8   0
15 x 11

CL

BATH #3

DRESSING AREA

SOAK

BATH #1
COFFERED CEIL.

CL

B.R. #2
6   0
12 x 12

LIN

B.R. #3
9   0
11 x 14

SEAT

U

BATH #2

CL

SECOND FLOOR PLAN

1539 SQ. FT. MAIN

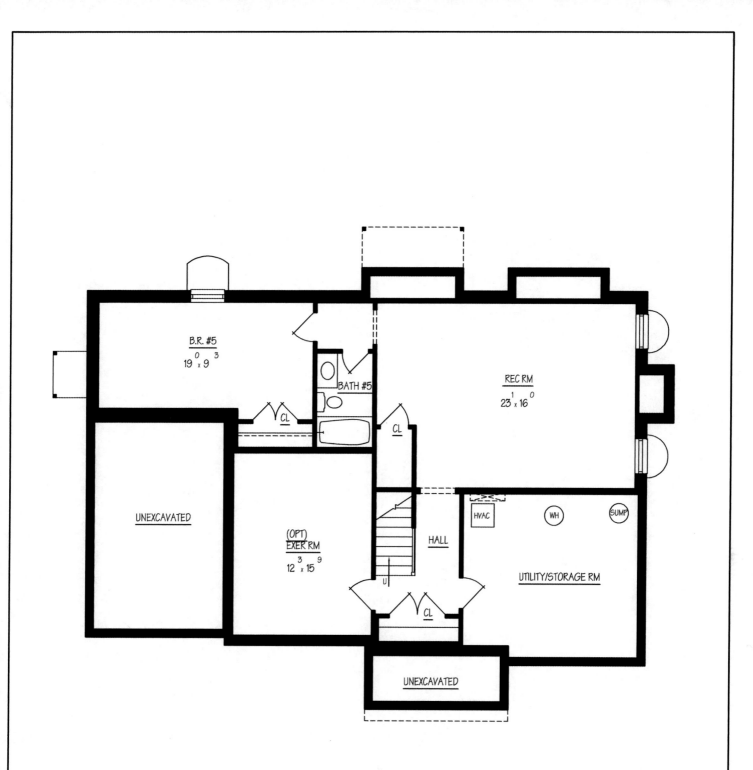

B.R. #5
19 ^{0} x 9 ^{3}

BATH #5

CL

REC RM
23 ^{1} x 16 ^{0}

CL

UNEXCAVATED

(OPT)
EXER RM
12 ^{3} x 15 ^{9}

HALL

HVAC

WH

SUMP

UTILITY/STORAGE RM

U

CL

UNEXCAVATED

BASEMENT PLAN

804 SQ. FT. FINISHED

Lionel Manufacturing Company
New York, New York
1903 - 1969

Joshua Lionel Cowen was born in New York City on August 25, 1877. An inventive and enterprising youth, Cowen started working in his teens for the Acme Electric Lamp Co. in Manhattan and found himself in the heart of a technological free-for-all. Electricity was being incorporated into everyday life, and would affect society henceforth. At the Acme Electric Lamp Co. Cowen was responsible for assembling battery lamps. In his spare time, he experimented and created variations of battery-operated lamps.

By 1901, Cowen was twenty-four years old and continuing his experiments. A local merchant approached him with the request that he produce a whimsical window display to attract the public. His first production was the "Electric Express," a showpiece featuring trains powered by a dry cell battery wired to the track. This was a grand departure from the wind-up, steam-powered or motorized vehicles of the time.

During this new era of a new century life in America seemed to be changing and advancing at an incredible rate. Transportation throughout the country was taking off, with railroad tracks crossing the country while trolley cars or streetcars were a staple in every major city. New York City had developed an elaborate transportation system of electrically powered streetcars. This became the model for Cowen's next production of displays. Once again, they were a huge hit. The orders started coming in from stores as far away as Rhode Island, and Joshua Lionel Cowen found himself in business.

In 1903, the Lionel Manufacturing Company was established. The company started by producing store displays featuring trains and trolley cars, but five years later realized there was a larger market for children's toys. It was for this market that the company could produce trains with movable working parts that captured the imaginations of children of all ages. In 1909, the company added the tag line "The Standard of the World" to all their promotional advertising.

While every other major train manufacturer around the world was producing trains with steam engines or wind-up clockwork mechanisms,

Identification Clues

- Examine the piece for the logo, which is usually easy to find. All the boxes are marked and some include graphics.

- Trains and cars are all marked with numbers that indicate the date manufactured. The lower the number on the engine, the earlier its production.

Above: This Lionel terrace with #124 station is complete with a waiting room mounted on an elaborate stepped platform, a railing and simulated lawn area containing a flag pole and ornamental flower pot. The piece dates from 1928-1930.

Lionel continued to perfect the electric train. Cowen understood the power of electricity and realized it would become the power of the future. In 1918 the company was renamed the Lionel Corporation and by 1920 it had become one of three major American producers of model electric trains and accessories. The company continued to grow and expand the line of engines, cars and accessories. In 1931 the company took over the financially failing Ives Company. The company took great pride in the trains produced, and looked to events in the world as inspiration for other toys.

Lionel trains were known for the use of a third rail and are marked

Lionel on the engine. Serial numbers were also assigned to engines. The lower the number the earlier the production. Trolley cars produced by Lionel are sought after by collectors because these pieces were produced for a limited time. The attention to detail and craftsmanship in production makes these sets collectible today.

The company continued to be prosperous until the mid-1950s when Cowen retired and sold his interest in the company. He died at the age of eighty-five, on September 8, 1965. In 1969 the company was sold to General Mills and a limited production of Lionel trains was resumed in Mount Clemons, Michigan.

Top: Trying to expand the company's appeal to girls, Lionel released this unsuccessful "0" gauge train set that consisted of a pink locomotive and tender, yellow and teal box cars, lavender hopper, pink canister car and a blue caboose. **Above:** This standard-gauge Lionel #400E steam locomotive and #400T tender was manufactured by the company between 1931-1937. Measuring 31 3/8 inches overall, this was one of the largest engines produced by the company.

Collector Alert

Look out for repainting or artificially distressed work on trains. There are companies making boxes today in the style and design of the boxes produced in the 1930s and 1940s.

This area of collecting is vast and collectors should seek out knowledgeable dealers or collectors for more information.

Top: This realistic train stop could be in Anytown, USA. It is a fine example of Lionel's use of color in the manufacturing of its train lines and of the diversity in the type of accessories available.
Left: In a continued attempt to enter the girls' toy market, Lionel introduced this well-constructed functioning replica of Mom's oven and stove made of porcelain and iron and complete with burners, gauges, backsplash, and electric cord for heating. It measured 32 inches high by 26 inches wide.

Top: This boxed Lionel #390E locomotive and tender, shown with its original box, was manufactured by the company from 1929-1931. Also shown are two Pullman cars; one observation car; one mail car; and two circuit breakers #91, all dating from the 1940s. **Right:** Like many companies, Lionel banked on the success of Disney's characters in making toys like this long-billed composition Donald Duck and Pluto hand car. The original box is shown in the inset photo.

Top: This tinplate standard-gauge Lionel bridge #300 in green has yellow tower ends and railings. It is in excellent condition and was made circa 1928. Above left: Lionel advertised its train sets in magazines like *Boy's Life* in 1931, left, and 1928, right. Left: This typical tinplate tender or coal car would ride behind the mighty Lionel locomotive.

 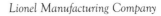

Top: The Lionel standard-gauge Blue Comet set is circa 1931-1934. It features a #400E loco-motive done in blue with a blue frame; #400 tender; a #420 "Faye" Pullman; a #421 Westpal Pullman and #422 "Temple" observa-tion car. **Above:** Lionel's electric trains were advertised in *Boy's Life* in 1929. **Above right:** Lionel's Santa hand car features Mickey Mouse peeking out of Santa's bag. The original box is shown in the inset photo. **Right:** This Lionel Peter Rabbit chick mobile hand car features a composition Peter and Easter Egg basket.

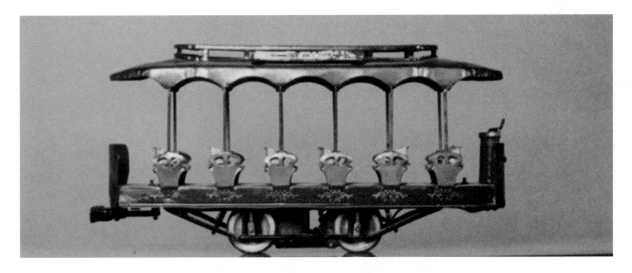

Top: A rare Lionel 390-E features copper domes; a side orange stripe; steel boiler and die-cast frame advertised as the Build-A-Loco Series. It is circa 1929-1931. **Above:** This Lionel 2 7/8-gauge hand-painted green-and-maroon electric transit car has six adjustable open bench seats and measures 15½ inches in length.

McLoughlin Brothers
New York, New York
1828 - 1920

Identification Clues

- Look for McLoughlin logo or label on the item
- Highly lithographed and colorful paper-on-wood items, puzzles, blocks and books

The company was founded in Brooklyn, New York, by John McLoughlin, Jr. and became the first company to mass-produce paper dolls and paper soldiers. Eventually McLoughlin expanded production to include dollhouse furniture, toy theatres with actors and scenery, blocks, games and children's books as well as a huge variety of paper toys. The toys are characterized by the use of color lithography. A family-controlled company, McLoughlin became the leading American publisher of such items by the 1880s. The company was sold to Milton Bradley in 1920.

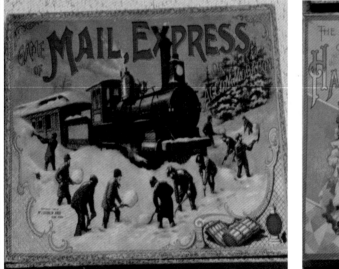

Above and right: Popular toys produced by McLoughlin Brothers circa 1895 included board games, blocks and puzzles.

Above and left: The company is known for its color lithography, which was also used to create elaborate dollhouses of lithographed collapsible cardboard.

Manoil Manufacturing Company, Inc.
Waverly, New York
1927 - 1955

Identification Clues

- Look for the Manoil company encircled M on the toys
- Early 1930s Manoil soldiers have a concave under base
- 1940s Manoil soldiers are on the portly side
- Late 1940s and 1950s soldiers are more realistic and leaner-looking
- Pre-World War II soldiers are marked with a numbering system on the toy: "M" and number between 1 - 169 Post-War items are marked "M" and numbered 170 - 224
- Manoil composition items are marked "MC" and numbered 1, 2, 3, 3a and 4
- Happy Farm Series of lead figures are marked "M" and 41/ and another number ranging from 1-41 depending on the figure

The land of opportunity and abundance became the United States moniker at the turn of the last century, as families traveled great distances to escape oppression in their home countries and to establish themselves on American soil. One such example was a Rumanian family with the surname of Manoil, who sailed into New York City harbor in the 1900s to stake their claim. The family settled in New York City, where they established their new life.

In 1927 Jack Manoil started a novelties and metal lamp manufacturing business located at 34 West Houston Street in New York City. The first company was named Jack Manoil Manufacturing, but the name changed a year later when older brother Maurice joined the company as co-owner. On July 28, 1928, it became known as the Man-

O-Lamp Corporation and continued to manufacture lamps for the next six years. In July 1934, however, the brothers made a lasting name change for their company, turning it into the Manoil Manufacturing Company, Inc.

Along with the name change in the 1930s came a departure from manufacturing lamps to a focus on toys, as well as a relocation to Brooklyn, New York, in 1937. Maurice handled the business end of the operations while Jack took the reins as creative director for the production of the toy line. The company's first toy line in 1934 consisted of four die-cast cars that were 4½ inches in length, a pair of sedan coupes and a die-cast wrecker. Jack employed the creative assistance of Walter Baetz, a Moravian from Canada, who ultimately became the company's

Above: Manoil made its name with the introduction of a platoon of lead soldiers in 1935. The figures were produced in a wide variety of poses.

longtime sculptor and designer. Working together, the two brought a greater diversity to the toy line. Jack and Walter often worked late into the night, perfecting their creations, and in 1935 they introduced the Manoil lead soldiers. The platoon of lead soldiers became popular and the creative duo was constantly looking for ways to perfect their molds to order to increase the structural soundness and eliminate the possibilities of air bubbles in the lead castings. These changes, mostly subtle and often even undetectable, account for any variations in the look and design of some of the soldiers from year to year.

In June of 1940, Waverly, New York, became the new home for Manoil Manufacturing. At its peak, the company employed two hundred and twenty-five people. The move to Waverly, which is just north of New York City, in Westchester County, proved to be an excellent decision. The new location provided the company with better access to the railroad line, which made shipments easier and affordable. But the overall prosperity and production of the company did not last long. The threat of a second world war prompted the United States government to prohib-

it the use of lead in the manufacturing of toys. The regulation stated: "No lead toys can be fabricated after April 1st (1942) and the quantity of lead used during the first quarter of 1942 must be restricted to 50 percent of the amount used in either the 3rd or 4th quarter of 1941." Toys made from other strategic material were able to be manufactured until June 30, 1942. The Manoil Manufacturing Company, Inc. responded to this mandate by temporarily shutting down production with the onset of World War II, but resumed a limited production of a sulfur-based fine-grained composition soldier in January of 1944. The toys proved to be brittle and ultimately unsuccessful, and production was terminated by year's end. The end of World War II brought about a rejuvenation in the Manoil offerings of several new lines of soldiers and the creation of its popular Happy Farm series, which reflected life in rural America. Despite the popularity of the new creations, distribution began to decline and the company was forced to move into a smaller Waverly location. In 1953 the company became know as the Jack Manoil Specialty Company, and finally went out of business with Jack Manoil's death in 1955.

Above left: A blacksmith from the "Happy Farm" series provided an alternative to military personnel in the Manoil line. **Top:** This cast-lead soldier operates a searchlight. **Above (1):** This Manoil metal cast cannon is shown with its original box. **Above (2):** The marking "USA "is often found on Manoil toys.

Märklin

Göppingen, Germany
1859

Identification
Clues
• Examine the piece for the
logo, which is usually
easy to find

This toy company is considered the most influential toy manufacturer in the world. Märklin set the standard for quality, design and aesthetics in the toy world. The craftsmanship and colorful history of this great toy maker has been unparalleled. Founded in 1859 by tinsmith Theodor Märklin and his wife Caroline in Göppingen, Germany, the company's first efforts were doll-sized tinplate kitchenware.

When their two sons took over the business in 1880 the company took off. Like other firms around the world, they often produced toys that reflected in miniature the changing world at the turn of the century. The Märklins seemed to perceive this world with extreme clarity and sharp focus. From the start, their attention to every detail right down to the spokes on the wheels set them apart from other toy makers. Their toys were bought by royalty and by wealthy families around the world. The production was vast and they explored every possible design for zeppelins; cars; trains; boats; carousels; and carriages.

The designs were nearly exact replicas of the full-size vehicles in fashion at the time, and the interior mechanisms were also quite superior to those in other company's toys. The clockwork mechanisms gave way to steam and eventually to electricity. These features were incorporated into the design of the toys without any sacrifice of beauty. In 1891 the company introduced the first standardized tinplate track for trains in Europe, which became known as standard gauge.

Above: This Märklin locomotive and tender has three passenger cars with roofs that open and close. It is shown with the original box. The set dates from the early 1900s.

Collector Alert

Look out for repainting or artificially distressed work on trains, boats and automobiles. This will devalue the piece. Some pieces have chipped or missing paint, which is okay provided other paint was not applied to the piece in an attempt to fix it up.

Top: Märklin produced a variety of accessories to accompany the locomotive, tenders and passenger cars. This elaborate station includes figures, lamps, fences and a pair of trains on the tracks. **Above left:** This early Märklin fire pumper has a copper bulb and black boiler with chain-driven gears that are activated by an intricate clockwork mechanism. **Left:** Märklin often placed advertising on its tinplate train cars. Each of these cars features different advertising.

Top: Most Märklin stations are elaborate in scale and very detailed. These were very popular with children. **Above:** This live steam engine is shown with its original box. **Above right:** Part of the mighty Märklin fleet of ocean vessels is this clockwork tinplate boat. **Right:** These tinplate tanker cars also feature advertising.

Louis Marx & Company
New York, New York
1919 - 1979

L ouis Marx was born in 1896 to German immigrants living in Brooklyn, New York. His father was a tailor. As Marx grew, he exhibited ambition and intelligence, which helped him to finish public school at age fifteen. A family friend introduced him to the toy company owner Ferdinand Strauss, who hired him as an office/errand boy. At his young age, Marx could not have realized the significance of landing a job with Strauss's mechanical toy company.

Over the next four years Marx worked hard and exhibited great promise. Strauss recognized his potential and in 1916 appointed him in charge of the East Rutherford, New Jersey, factory. He took on the challenge of running the factory and explored a variety of manufacturing possibilities. One of his ideas was that Strauss develop small retail stores to sell the company's toys. Marx encountered total resistance from Strauss and the board of directors on this notion, and believed in it strongly enough

that in 1917 he parted ways with Strauss.

Marx enlisted in 1917 to fight in World War I and one year later, rose to the rank of sergeant. Following the war, he went into business with his brother David. They worked together as agents between factories and wholesale jobbers. The economy after the war was booming and the brothers' business felt the effect of the boom. The demand for toys was on the increase. Louis Marx began to take more of an interest in the toys being produced. He analyzed the design, materials used and the overall structure and began to propose new economical ways to mass-produce the same toys. This saved money for the manufacturers, increased the output and doubled the production of toys, resulting in higher profits for the wholesalers. Because the brothers worked on commission, they saw profits on both sides. Marx's ambition grew to become the world's leading toy manufacturer.

Identification Clues
- Marx toys are marked MARX, or with the logo and company name
- Later toys made in Japan in the 1950s are marked Line-Mar

Above: Comic character toys dominated the Marx mechanical toy offerings. The company was one of the first to focus on attractive packaging as a means of helping sell their products.

Investing his savings, he bought old dies from his former employer, Strauss, and rented space in Erie, Pennsylvania, to begin toy production. He started out slowly and steadily, creating pieces for Strauss and Girard Model Works. Now that Marx was in charge, he could fulfill his dream of mass-production. It proved to be so successful that he became responsible for producing more than half of each company's production, and was able to place his logo on the toys. That is why today it is difficult to accurately identify Marx toys.

By 1928, toy companies were struggling to keep up the interest in their product lines. Marx decided to re-introduce one of the oldest toys around—the yo-yo. It is said he sold millions! It was all part of his strategy of mass-production volume selling, so he could supply the novelty stores, chain stores and the 5 & 10s with an abundance of his products.

This strategy allowed his company to weather the stormy Depression and helped Marx build his empire. As toy manufacturers around the country crumbled, Louis Marx was there to buy them out at a great price. It could be said that his yo-yo profits fueled his ambitions to acquire companies in America and in Europe. Marx always insisted on keeping costs down; he believed in the mass-production of toy manufacturing and always produced toys that directly reflected current events.

Top: This mechanical Toyland Milk wagon is shown with the original box. **Above:** This comic and colorful lithographed tinplate wind-up toy features Popeye with a parrot in a cage. **Right:** This lithographed tinplate Royal Bus, shown with its original box, is a wind-up toy.

Top: Dagwood, Superman and Pinocchio were popular tinplate wind-up toys manufactured by Marx. **Far left:** This Popeye Fliers tinplate mechanical toy, shown with its original box, features Popeye in one plane and Olive Oyl in the other. **Left:** When the Charlie McCarthy wind-up lithographed tinplate walker toy is wound it rocks back and forth and "walks" forward. **Above:** This streamlined speedway set has a snap-together race track and wind-up racing cars.

Louis Marx & Company

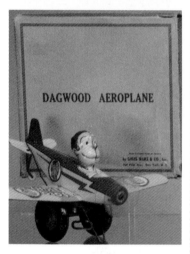

Top: This lithographed tinplate toy that features Charlie McCarthy and Mortimer Snerd is called "We'll Mow You Down." **Above:** This lithographed tinplate wind-up Dagwood aeroplane with original box is based upon the comic-strip "Blondie & Dagwood." **Right:** Marx produced numerous lithographed mechanical toys starring the lovable and popular Charlie McCarthy.

Top: An elaborate mountain village is the setting for this lithographed tin-plate mechanical toy by Marx, shown with the original box. **Above and left:** This pair of Mortimer Snerd toys is done in colorful tinplate lithography.

Top: Marx had great success with Pinocchio wind-up toys such as this example, and produced a broad variety to meet children's demands. **Above:** This is a lithographed tinplate wind-up version of the Mortimer Snerd Crazy Car. **Right:** The Popeye Express toy features a mechanical train and airplane along with the images of the members of the Popeye Gang.

Top: This Popeye The Champ toy, shown with the original box, features a lithographed tinplate base and celluloid figures. **Above left:** When this lithographed tinplate Popeye and Olive Oyl Jiggers toy is wound, Popeye dances and Olive moves around as though she is playing the accordion. **Above:** Charlie McCarthy stars again on Marx's lithographed tinplate mechanical Charlie McCarthy Crazy Car. **Left:** Equally popular were Marx's Popeye toys, such as this Popeye Pilot, shown with the original box.

Meccano Ltd.
Liverpool, England
1901 - 1980s

In order to understand the history of metal construction sets, we must journey across the ocean to Liverpool, England, where Frank Hornby patented his invention as the world's first metal construction set in 1901, and called it Meccano. The success of his new toy creation was immediate and its popularity widespread, so he decided to name his company after his invention, and Meccano Ltd. was born. The expanding arm of Hornby's construction empire branched out, with subsidiaries operating in Bobigny, France, and, until 1928, in New Jersey, United States.

The Meccano sets consisted of half-inch-wide tinplate strips that also included wheels and rods that could be connected to holes in the strips to create working models. The sets were later improved when the tinplate strips began to be manufactured with nickel-plated steel. In 1926 the company introduced red-and-green colored metal strips.

Meccano was responsible for creating a spring-driven locomotive in 1915 that, in turn, sparked Frank Hornby's future creativity in designing a completely separate line of toys, Hornby trains. The trains became popular in England in their own right after 1920, and in 1933 Hornby was responsible for introducing to the world a line of die-cast cars known as Dinky Toys.

During this period Meccano also expanded its construction toy kits to include a Constructor Plane set and the Motor Car Constructor set. The company continued to flourish and grow after Frank Hornby's death in 1936. The company was taken over by Lines Brothers in 1964, but trouble thereafter led to a halt in production in the early 1980s.

Above left: This colorful lithographed cardboard sign was used as a counter display to sell the Meccano automobile construction kits. **Above right:** This vivid cardboard box comes from the Meccano motor car construction kits.

Left: This lithographed cardboard sign features a boy working on Meccano's Eiffel Tower construction kit. **Top:** This lithographed cardboard counter sign advertises the airplane construction kit. **Above:** The automobile construction kits were produced in a variety of colors.

Meccano Ltd. 181

Merrythought Ltd.
Ironbridge, England
1919

Identification Clues

- In the first year of production only, the embroidered label omits the words "Hygienic Toys"

- Toys produced in the late 1930s have pewter buttons in the ears

- Bears and toys produced prior to 1939 feature woven cloth tag on feet of bears and dolls that reads:

  Merrythought
  Hygienic Toys
  Made in England

- Bears and toys produced after WWII have a printed cloth foot tag that reads:

Founders W.G. Holmes and G.H. Laxton started out with a small spinning mill producing mohair from imported raw mohair. With the advent of cheaper, synthetic mohair production as competition, the company diversified into manufacturing soft toys and bears, opening a factory in 1930 at Coalbrookdale, which is now called Ironbridge because it is the sight of the first iron bridge constructed in 1779. Holmes and Laxton eventually hired a former employee of the Chad Valley factory as production director and a former employee of J.K. Farnell as sales director. The company's first catalog appeared in 1931, featuring designs by Florence Atwood, former designer at Chad Valley, who stayed with Merrythought as chief designer until her death in 1949. The name Merrythought, which they took on when they began producing mohair toys, means wishbone in old English, and the wishbone became the company's logo.

The company produced teddy bears; soft toy animals; nightwear cases; rattles and flexi-toys; and, in 1933, dolls, which by 1937 had evolved from simple babies to articulated felt figures similar to those made by the nearby Chad Valley and the Italian Lenci. Large riding toys were also added to the line in 1933. The Bingie family of teddy bears was especially popular in the 1930s. Florence Atwood designed Merrythought's first panda in 1939, after the panda Ming had come to stay at the London Zoo. The company also manufactured characters like the golliwog, Dinkie, Bonzo and, under license from MGM, Jerry Mouse and later, Tom and Jerry.

Above left: This circa-1932 Merrythought teddy, part of the company's Magnet bear series, is art silk, a manmade material meant to replace mohair. The material was not widely accepted and was only used for a short time. The red color is rare for this company. Note the cloth label on the left foot. **Above right:** A slightly later bear, this 14-inch golden mohair teddy dates from the 1940s. It features the typical Merrythought claw design; again the cloth label is on the left foot.

Metalcraft Corporation
St. Louis, Missouri
1920 - 1940s

The first toys from this company, then known as Metallic Industries, were playground equipment and sidewalk toys. The success of a teeter-totter toy called the teeter-go-round earned the company membership in the Toy Manufacturers of America after only one year in the toy business. This early recognition helped push the design team to develop more than a dozen different offering for the next year. Some popular pieces were the Taxi-plane, Winsumcoaster and Jackrabbit racer. After an initial boom, sales began to decline; the company renamed itself Metalcraft and looked for a new product to capture the buying public's interest. The year was 1927 and Lindbergh had just successfully completed his transatlantic flight from New York to Paris. This international event caught the attention of the media around the world, while manufacturing companies scrambled to capture the rights to produce a "Lindy" airplane toy.

Metalcraft obtained the rights to manufacture a "Spirit of St. Louis" pressed-steel airplane kit. Once again the company struck gold. Each kit was

manufactured in a variety of sizes, and contained one basic airplane with parts for assembling any number of airplane styles. The variety of parts captured the child's imagination for hours and made the kit extremely popular. They sold by the thousands, but the novelty soon began to wear off, and by 1928 Meatalcraft went back to full production of scooters, wagons, and tricycles—also known as sidewalk toys. These were staple production items, but the company continued to search for another concept that would duplicate the tremendous success of the "Lindy" toy.

Looking around the marketplace, Metalcraft understood that the increased costs associated with the production of cast-iron toys were the result of the sales decline in that area. However, the most popular selling toys were pressed-steel trucks made by Buddy L. Metalcraft's facilities were already producing steel sidewalk toys, so company executives knew there had to be a way to manufacture affordable toys with the quality of Buddy L's products. This was the challenge. To meet it, Metalcraft devised a scaled-

Identification Clues

- Trucks with advertising
- Early trucks feature wooden disc wheels
- Automobiles and trucks have sleek deco designs

Above: Metalcraft's Coca-Cola truck is made from the company's signature pressed steel and features glass bottles and disc wheels. Coca-Cola was one of the first companies with which Metalcraft contracted for its advertising trucks.

down version of a steel truck designed to carry advertising on the panels of the truck. In order to keep the prices down, the pieces had to be manufactured in large number. Metalcraft obtained initial contracts with Kroger Stores, the Jewel Tea Company and Coca-Cola. Once again the company had found a niche in the marketplace and sales grew. Production of these advertising premium toys soon outgrew the staple production of sidewalk toys.

The premium market was not limited to toy trucks. Metalcraft also produced premiums that were popular at drug and grocery stores. These included painted pressed-steel folding chairs and a four-wheeled, 32-inch-by-16-inch coaster wagon. The wagon was the largest premium produced by the company and was awarded to the customer who presented the store with a fully punched card for the purchase of a dog food called "Doggie Dinner" plus 99 cents. The trucks dominated the production line and by 1932, Metalcraft claimed to have produced more than a million "busi-

ness leaders," as it affectionately referred to its trucks.

Always trying to stay on top of technology, Metalcraft began experimenting with battery-operated trucks. The company took a gamble and mass-produced this new creation, which they planned to add to the premium line. Unfortunately, the company's clients rejected the toys, which left Metalcraft with a huge inventory to sell. They tried to regain old contracts in the wholesaler and jobber market by hiring agents to effectively market their products. As the number of employees increased, Metalcraft had to raise prices for their toys at a time when other toy manufacturers around the country were slashing theirs to maintain a competitive edge. The company struggled along for a few years, but sales steadily declined. The poor economy restricted the company from reorganizing and in 1937 Metalcraft stopped production for good. The company known for its great ideas was finally unable to reinvent itself.

Above: Metalcraft referred to its pressed-steel trucks with advertising on their panels, such as this Shell Motor Oil truck, as "business leaders." By 1932, the company claimed to have produced more than one million of these.

Left: Metalcraft's production of advertising premium trucks included a large variety of companies. The trucks were so popular that this line soon exceeded Metalcraft's staple production of sidewalk toys. **Above:** In December 1928 Metalcraft advertised some of its other toys in *Child Life* magazine.

Ohio Art
Bryan, Ohio
1908

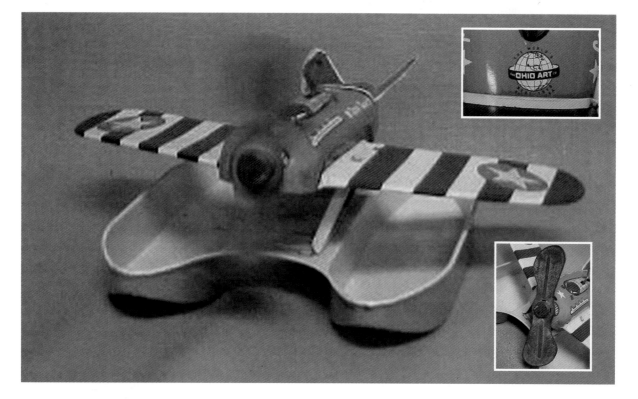

Toy production remained primarily domestic until the 1900s, when Germany began exporting toys so cheaply that many American manufacturers couldn't compete. The import of toys and games totaled about three million dollars in 1900; by 1914 imports had captured half of the market. During the years leading up to World War I, toy manufacturers experienced reductions in materials used in the toy production. With the declaration of war by the United States on Germany on April 6, 1917, drastic restrictions were placed on the toy industry. At this point, the Toy Manufacturers of America (TMA) formed a lobbying group in Washington, DC, and convinced Congress that despite the war, American children were entitled to toys and playthings made by domestic companies. The TMA pushed for a 75 percent tariff on all imports. This legislation strengthened the domestic companies and eased the way for other fledgling companies to make a profit.

Ohio Art was one of the companies that benefited from this legislation. It had been founded in 1908 by a dentist, H.S. Winzeler, who was entrepreneurial by nature, and also owned a grocery business. His initial idea was to create metal picture frames for works of art, hence the name of the company. In 1908 his creations were being sold in Sears, Kresge's and other stores around the country.

In March 1917 Ohio Art purchased the Erie Toy Plant and entered the toy business. Among the company's early creations was a galvanized tin windmill. Ohio Art progressed to manufacturing items for other companies, such as a climbing monkey on a string for Ferdinand Strauss. Eventually Winzeler sold the Erie Toy Plant to toy giant Louis Marx. Even though Ohio Art was originally as a frame company, the firm continues to manufacture toys today in Ohio, and has introduced a variety of tin toys, tea sets, sand pails and shovels. The company's 1960 introduction of the Etch-A-Sketch toy, however, ensured that Ohio Art will forever leave its mark on American popular culture.

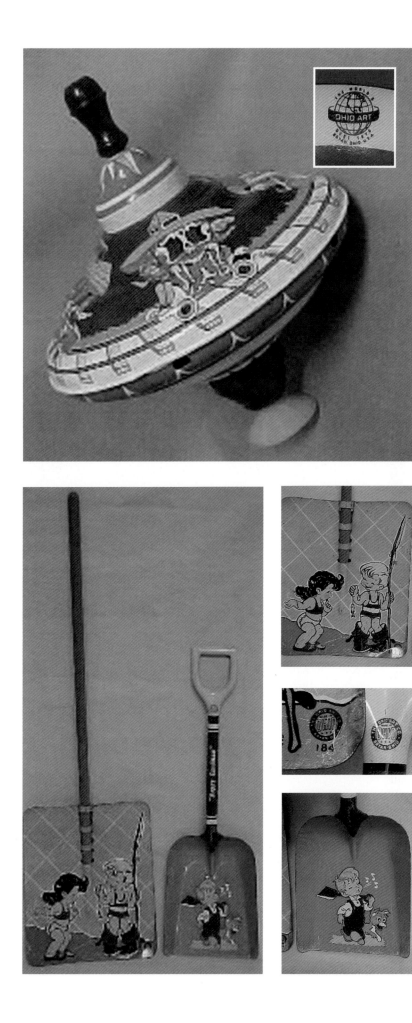

Collector Alert

Keep items out of direct sunlight or fading will occur. These toys will rust easily so keep out of damp or humid environments. Since these toys were played with in the sand and left outdoors, it is common to find them in less-than-desirable condition.

Top left: A colorful lithographed tinplate top was Ohio Art's version of this childhood favorite. **Far left and left:** Ohio Art produced a variety of lithographed tinplate sand shovels. **Top:** A popular beach toy from the company was this sandpail and shovel set. **Above(1):** This lithographed tinplate globe still bank has a slot on top for inserting coins. **Above (2):** This Sheriff Derringer pocket pistol cap gun, shown in its original packaging, is made of die-cast metal.

Pratt & Letchworth

Buffalo, New York

1880s - 1900

Identification Clues

- Most of the horse-drawn vehicles found today were produced by Pratt & Letchworth

- Look for quality casting and fine detail around the windows of the vehicle, the horses and the painting of any figures

Credited with being one of America's largest manufacturers of cast-iron objects at the end of the nineteenth century, Pratt & Letchworth was founded by Samuel F. and Pascal P. Pratt together with William P. Letchworth. This cast-iron manufacturing company originally produced carriage and truck hardware under the formal company name of the Buffalo Malleable Iron works.

Around 1890 Francis Carpenter sold his toy business to Pratt & Letchworth, along with the patent rights. The company redesigned the look of the toys, resulting in very few examples that looked anything like the Francis Carpenter toys. The toy business enhanced Pratt & Letchworth's core business of providing material for the booming expansion of American transportation. Along with cast-iron fire toys, artillery wagons, wheeled vehicles and toy trains, the company also produced real parts for locomotives and automobiles. But as costs rose along with a consumer demand for updated products that reflected the changing times, the company ceased toy production in 1900.

Top: This cast-iron surrey, circa 1900, has spoke wheels and is pulled by one horse. Above: This rare cast-iron clockwork mechanism locomotive and tender has a cowcatcher, lamp and bell.

W. S. Reed Toy Company
Leominster, Massachusetts
1875 - 1897

This company became known for its lithographed paper-on-wood pull toys. The colorful lithography became its trademark. In addition to the pull toys, they made blocks and construction sets, as well as: Ocean Waves, a clipper ship pull toy (1877); a circus wagon with a pair of horses (1878); the United States Capital Construction set (1884); and cast-iron mechanical banks.

Concepts for mechanical bank design hit designers in the strangest of places. William S. Reed was inspired to create the design for the "Old Woman In The Shoe" cast-iron mechanical bank while attending a church service.

The company was granted a patent for the design on November 27, 1883, and manufactured the toy bank. This is the only patented design the company was granted and there are only two known examples in the world—which makes this an extremely rare bank

Reed's original design and final patent for a "Toy Money Box" included wheels on the base of the bank and planned for the woman's left arm to move up and down. But during this period, manufacturers often varied patent concepts when production costs were considered high. This was the case with Reed's design, so the bank was cast without wheels.

Identification Clues

- Toys are marked "W. S. Reed Toy Co." with patent date also marked on the box or on a paper label on the toy itself

Above left: The Old Woman in the Shoe mechanical bank set a new world record at auction for a mechanical bank in May 1998 when it was hammered down for $426,000. **Above:** The "America" clipper ship is a lithographed-paper-on-wood sailing vessel with outstanding graphics depicting a wood-grain finish, port holes and sea splash.

A. Schoenhut Company
Philadelphia, Pennsylvania
1872 - 1935

This company has a long and distinctive history. It was founded by a German immigrant who arrived in America shortly after the Civil War. Albert Schoenhut arrived in Philadelphia and secured employment with John Deiser & Sons, who imported a variety of items from Europe, in particular from Germany. Schoenhut found his niche with the company by learning to repair all the toy pianos that were imported from Germany. This inspired him to found his own company that would create toy pianos of high quality. In 1872, A. Schoenhut began to produce toy pianos. The Schoenhut toy pianos were complete, well-built and, unlike those manufactured by his competition, produced a pleasant, on-pitch tone. In fact the pianos were so popular that the company did not produce anything other than pianos until 1903.

That year the Schoenhut Company expanded their line to include a variety of wooden toys, including the Humpty Dumpty Circus. The circus set was simple, made up of only a few pieces and soared in popularity. Schoenhut increased production of the set and went on to produce a vari-

Above: Schoenhut's carved wooden dolls, first made in 1911, were noteworthy for their spring-jointed bodies, which allowed them to take on a variety of lifelike poses. The dolls shown here have wigs; other examples had carved hair.

ety of accessories, such as wooden figures of a ringmaster; acrobats; a lion tamer; animals; clowns; and ladders. All the pieces for the early sets were hand-carved wood.

In addition to the popular circus set, Schoenhut also produced dolls; boats; toy guns; blacks; shooting galleries; horse-drawn carriages; dollhouses; and dollhouse furniture. Schoenhut's dolls, first made in 1911, were noteworthy for their spring-jointed bodies, which allowed them to take on a variety of lifelike poses. The joints were advertised as having "Steel spring hinges having double tensions and swivel connections," instead of the standard rubber cords used for jointing. The dolls also had two holes in the soles of each foot, into which posts of accompanying metal stands were fitted, allowing the dolls to stand erect.

Wooden jointed comic strip characters such as Felix, Barney Google, Sparkplug and Maggie and Jiggs, were also popular Schoenhut creations.

Top: Among the company's best-known toys is The Humpty Dumpty Circus, which is shown here complete with big top, backdrop, circus animals and performers made of carved wood. **Above:** The pig, farmer and cow are carved-wood examples of the farm series Schoenhut created to expand the popular circus series. **Above right:** Carved-wood circus performers included this lady standing on horseback.

Top: Nursery-rhyme and comic-strip characters were also represented in Schoenhut's toy line. Shown here, from left to right, are (top row): Barney Google and Spark Plug; Mary and her lamb; (bottom row) ring master and elephant; a cage wagon with lion from the Humpty Dumpty Circus; and the comic-strip duo Maggie and Jiggs. **Above:** This carved-wood poodle still has its original box. **Right:** The popular Schoenhut wooden child's piano has a pair of ornately cast candle stick holders and two cast support legs, as well as the company decal.

Top: This acrobat set consists of two bisque-headed tightrope performers, two female performers, a Chinaman, a hobo and a clown. **Above left and left:** Individually boxed carved-wood animals were available individually to add to the Humpty Dumpty Circus sets. These are shown with the original boxes. **Above:** A variety of Schoenhut toys were featured in this December 1928 ad in *Child Life* magazine.

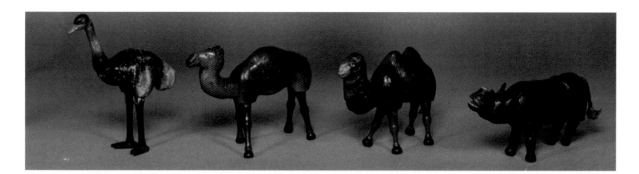

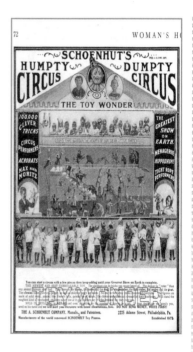

Top, above and right: Schoenhut advertised a variety of toys, including its wooden circus animals, in many magazines, including the December 1907 issue of *Woman's Home Companion*, shown above. **Above right:** Schoenhut issued numerous catalogs for its various toy lines.

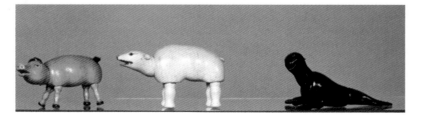

Top, above left and left: Schoenhut's colorful clowns and wooden animals were favorite additions to the Humpty Dumpty Circus. **Above:** The company's dolls, pianos and other toys were advertised in the December 1923 issue of *Pictorial Review.*

Schuco
Nuremberg, Germany
1912 - 1976

Identification Clues

- Bears made in the 1920s have folded paper tags hanging on their chests
- Bears made after World War II wear a red plastic tag affixed by a red bow
- Metal-wheeled bears usually had Schuco embossed on the wheels
- Cars made from 1930-1950 are marked Germany or U. S. Zone-Germany
- After World War II, the yes/no bear became known as Tricky

This German toy company, originally named Schreyer and Company, began operations when Heinrich Muller and Heinrich Schreyer teamed up to produce wind-up novelties. Muller had previous work experience with Bing, which gave the company an advantage in the marketplace.

Schuco soon established itself as one of the leaders in the wind-up toy category. They were on the brink of success when World War I broke out and both partners were conscripted. After the war, Adolph Kahn replaced Muller as Schreyer's partner and the company became known as Schuco. This name was added to the logo, a tumbling man clasping his feet, in 1921.

That same year, the company created what is probably its best known toy: the yes/no bear, which turned its head from left to right and nodded up and down when its tail was moved. This simple creation became a huge success for the company. Not only children, but adults, too, enjoyed the bears. This realization prompted Schuco to take the adult market more seriously, and create bears that doubled as perfume bottles, compacts and purses. The company also became known for the wind-up mechanisms in the automobile sets, character toys and motorcycles.

Above, left and right: This 3-inch mohair two-faced Janus bear was named after the Roman city god with two faces. This little bear still has the US Zone Germany tag intact.

Collector Alert

Schuco toys are very popular and can often be found at auction, flea markets or garage sale. Be sure all the parts are included in car sets. Keys are important, though they add more to the aesthetic value than to the monetary value.

Top and above: Schuco manufactured a variety of wind-up automobiles, including bsic sedans and snazzy convertibles. The company's vehicles were sold in attractive boxes, like the one pictured.

Above: Some of Schuco's wind-up automobiles included figures. **Right:** The company also became important for its stuffed animals and teddy bears. This oversized mohair bear has cardboard backing behind the felt foot pads.

Above: Schuco was known for its innovative novelty toys, such as this colorful wind-up Juggling Clown, shown with its original box. **Left:** This circa-late-1920s mohair-and-felt Schuco Yes/No bellhop bear has the rare felt boot design.

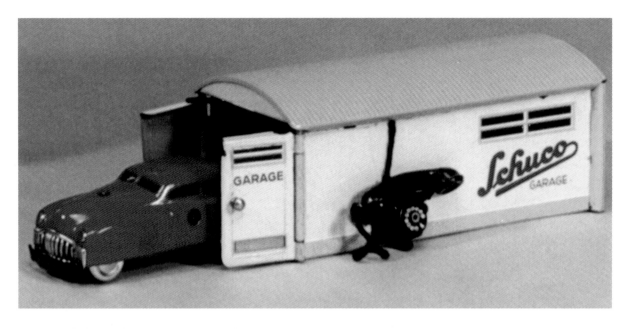

Top, above and right: In addition to numerous wind-up vehicles and accessories, Schuco produced a variety of accompanying sets, such as the garage and café shown here.

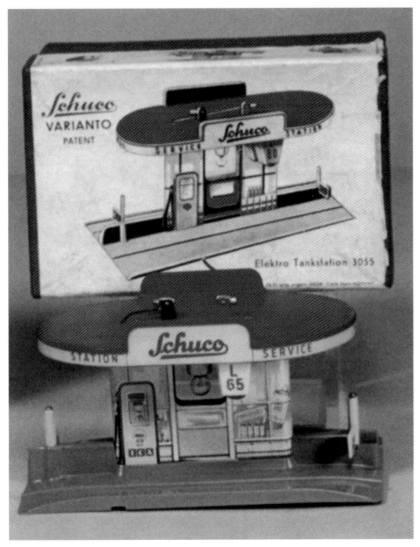

Above: This extension-ladder construction truck has a swinging platform, nickel levers and clockwork mechanism. **Left:** An electric service station is shown with its original box. When the nozzle of the pump is inserted into the car, the battery is recharged.

Above: Schuco's felt-and-mohair Yes/No bellhop monkey was a popular toy in the 1930s. **Right:** Monkeys were a favorite subject for the company's toys, and were made in a variety of materials and colors. This expressive pair is mohair.

Shepard Hardware Company

Buffalo, New York
1866 - 1892

Above: The cast-iron mechanical bank of Jonah and the Whale was patented in July 1890. When a coin is placed on Jonah's head and the lever is pressed, the man tosses Jonah forward and the whale's mouth opens. The coin slides off Jonah's head into the whale's mouth.

This company began producing cast-iron hardware supplies in the mid-1860's. Walter J. and Charles G. Shephard founded the company and in 1882 were granted a patent to manufacture cast-iron mechanical banks. They continued with the hardware supplies and featured the banks as novelties. The company was sold in 1892. Three Shepard Hardware Banks were later re-issued by J&E Stevens.

Identification Clues

- The coin traps on these mechanical banks were square and had to be opened with a key

- Only a few banks were produced by this company, including: Punch and Judy (1884); Trick Pony (1885) and Speaking Dog (1885)

Top: The Leap Frog cast-iron mechanical bank was designed by Peter Adams and patented in July 1890. When a coin is placed in the slot at the top of the stump, one boy leapfrogs over the other. His hand strikes a lever causing the coin to fall into the bank. **Above:** The Mason cast-iron mechanical bank was designed by Shepard and Adams and patented in February 1887. The hod carrier receives the coin, and throws it forward, depositing it in the bank as the mason rises and lowers the trowel. **Right:** The circa-1885 Picture Gallery cast-iron Mechanical Bank features a figure in the center who receives the coin in his hand and deposits it in the bank. All the letters of the alphabet and numbers from 1-26 are shown in rotation along with twenty-six different animals or objects with a short word for each letter.

Top left: The Uncle Sam cast-iron mechanical bank was patented in June 1886. When a coin is placed in the hand and the small knob on top of the box is pressed, the arm lowers and opens the satchel to receive the coin; the lower jaw of the figure keeps moving. **Top right:** The Stump Speaker cast-iron mechanical bank was patented in November 1886. **Above:** The Circus cast-iron mechanical bank was patented in February 1887. A coin is pushed into the slot when the crank is turned, and the clown and pony cart go around in a circle. **Left:** The Humpty Dumpty cast-iron mechanical bank was patented in June 1884. A coin is placed in the hand and when the lever is pressed, the arm is raised, allowing the coin to be deposited in the clown's mouth as the tongue falls back and the eyes roll forward. All these banks were designed by Charles Shepard and Peter Adams.

Top left: The Punch & Judy cast-iron mechanical bank was patented in July 1884. A coin is placed on the plate and when the button is pressed, Punch rushes forward and Judy turns quickly and deposits coin. **Top right:** Most mechanical banks came with colorful lithographed trade cards, which salesmen used to show the bank to prospective buyers, so the salesmen would not have to carry the heavy toys. **Above:** The Trick Pony cast-iron mechanical bank was designed by Julius Mueller and patented in June 1885. The pony receives the coin in his mouth and deposits it in the manger. **Right:** The Mason bank can be found today in several color variations, and with varying amounts of wear.

Simon & Halbig
Gräfenhain, Germany
1869 - 1920

Collector Alert

Check bisque for hairline cracks or peppering (black flecks) from the firing process. This will decrease the value of the doll. Excellent reproductions of antique porcelain dolls, including Simon & Halbigs, have been made by doll artists over the past few decades. These are usually appropriately marked, so be sure to check the markings on the back of the neck or on the back. As with most French and German porcelain dolls, Simon & Halbig's marking system is complex and must be studied. Collectors who do familiarize themselves with the markings can often learn a great doll about the doll in question from its marks. Many excellent reference books have been published about this area of collecting. Remember that Simon & Halbig marked all the heads they made, including those made for other doll manufacturers, so their mark does not guarantee the maker of the entire doll.

The factory was originally established to produce a variety of superior quality porcelain decorative items and soon began to specialize in producing bisque doll heads for the growing number of companies producing dolls. The company took great care and attention with every minor detail of the production, and become the second-largest manufacturer of bisque doll heads in Germany. Major doll manufacturers such as Kämmer & Reinhardt, Heinrich Handwerck, Cuno & Otto Dressel and even French companies like Jumeau and Roullet & Decamps recognized the superior craftsmanship and had Simon & Halbig produce heads for their dolls. This can make identification and dating the dolls difficult, as Simon and Halbig marked the heads they produced whether they were for their own dolls or for those of other companies.

This popularity and quality resulted in Siman & Halbig being taken over by Kämmer & Reinhardt in 1920 and mass-producing even more pieces than any other doll company at the time. This is also evident today; when you go to a doll show or an auction you will see more dolls with the Simon & Halbig mark than with any other manufacturer's name.

Identification Clues

- Dolls are incised with the name Simon & Halbig along with a mold number
- A DEP mark on the head indicates the doll was produced after 1887
- The SH mark indicates dolls made before 1905
- The S & H mark indicates dolls made after 1905

S H

DEP

S H

Germany

Above: This bisque-headed open-mouth child with full cheeks displays the typical characteristics of dolls produced by the prolific Simon & Halbig in the 1880s.

Steelcraft (J.W. Murray Manufacturing Company)
Cleveland, Ohio
1920s - 1940s

Above: Among Steelcraft's child-size cars was this pressed-steel Cadillac pedal car with black fenders and running boards. The car features a chrome grill and ornament; headlamps; a spotlight mounted on a stand; windshield; steering wheel and white upholstered seat.

During the 1920s airplanes shared the spotlight with a short-lived but distinctive airship, the zeppelin. A number of toy companies seized the opportunity to create toys that emulated the Graf Zeppelin, the Los Angeles and the Akron. Companies such as Marx, Strauss and Dent manufactured their airships in lead, iron and tin. Steelcraft's version was made from pressed steel. The J.W. Murray Manufacturing Company branched out from its traditional product line of stamped metal body parts for the automotive industry and introduced its first line of all-steel toys in the mid-1920s. The toys were made at the Murray, Ohio, manufacturing plant located in Cleveland, Ohio. This division of the company was known as Steelcraft.

The company concentrated pro-duction on pull toys and pedal cars. The pedal cars were pressed-steel, modeled after the full-scale GMC trucks, all with open cabs, and averaged 26 inches in length. In 1926, the company changed the design to imitate the life-size Mack trucks that were gaining public popularity. The quality and crafts-manship of the Steelcraft products provided stiff competition to Buddy L and Keystone, which also produced pressed-steel toys. The Steelcraft reputation for quality reached retail giants J.C. Penney and Sears, both of which requested their own "house brands" of pressed-steel toys. "Little Jim Playthings" was branded for J.C. Penney and "Boycraft" became the brand for Sears. The company continued to manufacture toys and pedal cars up to the outbreak of World War II. After the war, the company manufactured only pressed-steel pedal cars and bicycles.

Top: This Steelcraft pressed-steel tank truck has a filler cap on the top of the tank and disc wheels with solid rubber tires. Above: A scarce find, this Steelcraft pressed-steel truck has a Marion decal on the crane housing and a decal on door that reads "Mack - J.C. Penney." It also has red double-disc wheels and rubber tires.

Top: The Steelcraft convertible touring pedal car has curved fenders and running boards, a chrome grill and hood ornament. This magnificent car is more than 62 inches in overall length.
Right: The pressed-steel tank truck was produced in several color variations. This example has a black metal frame with red tank.

Top: This oversized pressed-steel US Mail Plane has a wingspan of 22½ inches. It displays typical signs of rust and play wear. Above: The company's pressed-steel flatbed dump truck has disc wheels and solid rubber tires. Left: Still another variation of the pressed-steel tank truck, this example has a black-and-red frame with red tank.

Margarete Steiff GmbH
Giengen, Germany
1880

Identification Clues

- Examine the piece for the button in the left ear of the bear or animal. The variations in the buttons can help in identifying the period of production, as follows.
  1904 on: Embossed elephant with upright trunk
  1905–1909: Blank button
  1905-1940: STEIFF printed in raised letters with a trailing underline of the final F
  1946–1947: Silver-blue dull blank button
  1948–1960: Silver button with Steiff in raised script
  1960–1976: Silver button with Steiff incised in script
  1977–Present: Brass button with Steiff incised in script
  1926–Present: Chest tags on all toys

- If there is no button in the left ear, check for a hole indicating where a button may have originally been placed

Margarete Steiff was born in 1847. Afflicted with polio as a baby, she spent the rest of her life in a wheelchair. She did not allow her infirmities to dampen her industrious spirit, and became an accomplished seamstress with her own dressmaking company, who made animals from remnant pieces of felt for the children in the neighborhood. A felt elephant pincushion became a favorite and she created it in larger quantities for sale in 1880.

Thus did Margarete Steiff, with the help of her brother Fritz and, eventually, Fritz's children, establish the Margarete Steiff Toy Company, devoted to the production of felt toys. In the early 1900s her nephew,

Richard, who was an accomplished artist and a longtime lover of bears, convinced his aunt to produce a jointed bear of his design, a kind of "bear doll." When the toy was introduced at the Leipzig Spring Fair in 1903 the overall reception was mixed; some even ridiculed the toy. However at the conclusion of the fair, an American buyer from George Borgfeldt noticed the bear and ordered three thousand pieces on the spot. While the order is known to have been filled and shipped, there is no further record of these bears.

Still the Steiff company persevered in perfecting its bear design, and by 1906 the so-called teddy bear was the company's best-seller. (Ideal

---

Above: The name Steiff is known first and foremost among teddy bear lovers. The company has produced teddy bears since the earliest years of the twentieth century. A typical Steiff teddy of its era, this circa 1920s fully jointed mohair bear has shoe-button eyes, a stitched nose and felt paw pads.

Behind The Scenes

The desirability of Steiff bears, animals and character dolls, which has always been high, continues to increase. Occasionally, however, these toys still turn up in unsuspected settings like garage sales and flee markets. A collector I met at an *Antiques Roadshow* appraisal session in San Francisco, California, showed me a bear she had acquired more than five years earlier from a dealer who knew the bear was rare, but did not realize how the bear market would rise over the course of time.

The white mohair Steiff "rod" bear came with a set of x-rays that exposed the metal rod joints. The bear featured a sealing-wax nose, was fully jointed and measured over 20 inches high. The collector had focused her collection on unusual Steiff bears and animals and had thus been attracted to the "rod" bear. The white color and rarity of this type of bear makes it a wonderful addition to any collection. My opinion of the bear's value was $20,000-$30,000.

and Steiff both claim to have created the first teddy bear, though Steiff's connection to Teddy Roosevelt is not as well documented as Ideal's.) Steiff continued to successfully produce teddy bears in a variety of styles, as well as animals of nearly every known type, and felt dolls of very fine craftsmanship and excellent quality. The company obtained a license to produce Mickey and Minnie Mouse in Germany in 1931, and also produced the German comic-strip characters Max and Moritz and their friends from Wilhelm Busch's popular cartoons, beginning in 1909. Its dolls were all felt, with a seam down the center of the face, and represented sailors, soldiers, clowns and a wide variety of nationalities, such as Native Americans and Eskimos.

From the earliest years the company marked its pieces with a button in the left ear, which helps to identify a Steiff. For all the myriad toys this German company has produced, it is best-known for its teddy bears, which it continues to produce, along with a large variety of animals, on its original grounds in Germany.

Above left: Steiff was an active toy company prior to the creation of the teddy bear. Among its earliest animals were dancing bears, which reflected the popular European fashion of muzzled bears led by a chain to dance in town squares. This 13-inch roly poly on a wooden base dates from 1898.

Above: This jungle is filled with mohair Steiff animals with detailed expressions, all circa 1940s and 1950s. **Right:** These felt cat and dog skittles have shoe-button eyes and wooden bases.

Collector Alert

The most valuable and vulnerable part of the bear is the nose or muzzle area. If there has been any restoration or damage in this area the value is affected. The pads should be felt and the nose hand stitched. Horizontal nose stitching indicates an early bear.

There are many reference materials on this popular company. A serious collector should consult as many as possible before acquisition.

Above: This trio represents the earliest teddy bears made by the company. From left: the 18-inch golden bear stuffed with kapok is circa 1905 and is jointed with paper discs and short metal rods; the 1904 excelsior-stuffed Bärle is 15 inches high and has paper disc joints with string and a sealing-wax nose; the grey 1905 Richard Steiff Bärle is 11½ inches high, has paper disc joints on short metal rods and a stitched nose. **Left:** Note the seam down the front of this felt gypsy doll's face as well as the individually sewn fingers.

Above: Steiff's collection of animals has always included lions and tigers and, of course, elephants. This group includes pieces as early as the 1913 mouse in the center; the others range in date from 1916 to 1948. The 11-inch-high elephant is circa 1930. **Right:** A mohair Steiff monkey posed for a publicity shot in the arms of a well dressed woman aboard a boat.

Above: From 1931 to 1936 Steiff had the German license to produce Mickey Mouse. Minnie was also made, starting in 1932; this example stands 8½ inches high. The Mickeys range from 6 to 15 inches high and are all early examples from 1931 and 1932. **Left:** This Steiff felt donkey on wooden wheels has shoe-button eyes and a leather saddle.

Above: In 1909 Steiff made the first Max and Moritz dolls based on Wilhelm Busch's popular cartoon. These two, center, are 12 inches high, circa 1910. Surrounding them, **from left**, are 17-inch-high characters: Uncle Fritz, Widow Bolte, Teacher Lampel, Mrs. Bock and Tailor Bock, all circa 1915-1917. **Right:** Other story-book characters rendered into felt included Dr. Heinrich Hoffmann's Struwwelpeter in 1912 (14 inches high) and Florence Upton's Golliwog in 1910 (13 inches high).

J. & E. Stevens Company
Cromwell, Connecticut
1843 - 1930s

John and Elisha Stevens were brothers from Cromwell, Connecticut who hold the distinction of being the first American mass-producers of metal toys. The brothers started out with a modest line of cast-iron hardware. Slowly they increased their production to include simple playthings, toy pistols, and gardening tools. Each year the company gained greater exposure for the high quality of its cast-iron offerings.

By 1870 the company was producing more than one thousand different items that included cast-iron doll furniture; stoves; toy cannons, cap guns; and tools. They even provided wheels and fittings for the Gong Bell Toy Company, which was located in the neighboring town. Making sure they hit every area, they produced their version of a bell toy, the Evening News Baby Quieter.

Despite the variety of items produced by J. & E. Stevens, only one item provided the company with international popularity: cast-iron mechanical banks. Their designs were clever, captivated children for hours, and taught valuable lessons about saving your pennies.

In 1869 Elisha Stevens left the company and formed the Stevens & Brown Manufacturing Company with George W. Brown, while his brother continued to make cast-iron hardware and toys, which Stevens & Brown distributed.

Identification Clues

- A lack of markings makes these toys and banks especially difficult to identify

- Collectors must familiarize themselves with the specific banks and toys made by the company

Above: The Boy Robbing Bird's Nest cast-iron mechanical bank dates from about 1906. A coin is placed on the tree limb and when the lever is pressed, the limb falls against the tree depositing the coin.

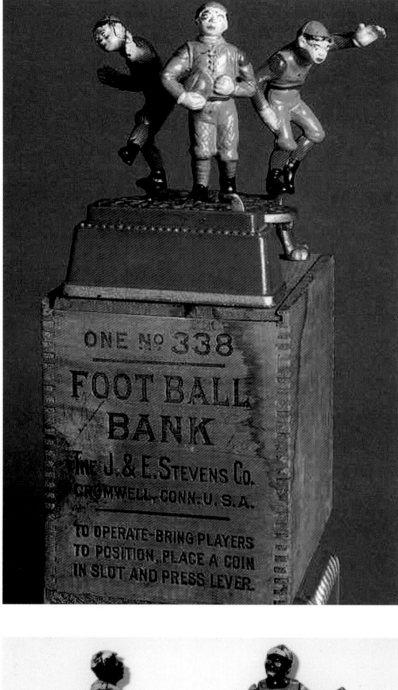

Above right: This cast-iron mechanical calamity bank, shown with its original wooden packing box was patented in July 1905. The right and left tackle are moved into position as shown; a coin is placed in the slot in front of the full back and the lever is pressed. The players swing together and touch heads, while the runner steps back and the coin drops into the bank.
Right: The Dark Town battery cast-iron mechanical bank was patented in January 1888. A coin is placed in the hand of the pitcher and when the lever is pressed, the coin is swiftly pitched, the batter swings and the coin is deposited by the catcher.

Top: From left, the cast-iron mechanical Girl Skipping Bank was patented in 1890; the Dentist cast-iron mechanical bank is circa 1880s and the Horse Race cast-iron mechanical bank was patented in August 1870. **Above left:** The Lion Hunter cast-iron mechanical bank, in which the figure bears a striking resemblance to Theodore Roosevelt, was patented in August 1911. A coin is placed in position in the barrel of the rifle. When the lever is pressed, the coin strikes the lion and falls into the receptacle below. **Left:** To operate the Indian Shooting Bear cast-iron mechanical bank, a coin is placed on the barrel of the rifle. When the lever is pressed, the coin hits the bear and is deposited into the bank.

Above: To operate the Boy Scout Camp cast-iron mechanical bank. a coin is placed on the tree above the tent. When the lever is pressed, the coin falls into the bank and the Boy Scout raises his flag. The Boy Scouts of America organization was founded in 1910 and chartered by Congress in 1916. **Right:** The Panorama cast-iron mechanical bank was patented in March 1876. The bank receives its name from the cylinders of pictures featured on the façade of the house. When a coin is deposited, a new picture rolls into view.

Top: The William Tell cast-iron mechanical bank was patented in June 1896. A coin is placed on the barrel of the riffle and when the right foot of the figure is pressed, the coin shoots the apple off the boy's head and is deposited into the bank. **Above:** This cast-iron Swan Chariot pull toy depicts a young girl seated in the shell-design seat of the open-winged swan. **Left:** To operate the circa-1885 Paddy and the Pig cast-iron mechanical bank, a coin is placed on the pig's nose. When the lever is pressed, the pig strikes the coin with its foot and the man's mouth opens to receive the coin.

Strauss Manufacturing Corporation
New York, New York
1900s - 1940s

Above: The Little Joe Socko Musical Bank is circa 1910-1920. The figure is made of white metal and the base is done in lithographed tin.

Ferdinand Strauss, an Alsatian immigrant, founded the corporation by importing toys and commissioning manufacturers from Germany to produce mechanical tin toys. Once the toys arrived in New York, Strauss printed his name on them, next to that of the German manufacturer, prior to distribution.

The onset of World War I in 1914 affected the importation of toys to America from Germany. Strauss reacted quickly and gathered a group of investors to establish his own manufacturing company in America, the Strauss Manufacturing Company, in 1914. He focused his toy line on mechanical tin toys with lots of action, which were very popular. By the late teens his designs had earned him the title: "founder of the mechanical toy industry in America." To retain control over the sale of his creations, he opened retail stores in four New York City railroad terminals.

Strauss continued to operate the manufacturing of toys and the retail sale of the pieces he was producing through 1932, when he sold the manufacturing interests. He maintained the operation of his profitable retail outlets, however, and retained a presence in the toy world by consulting for other toy manufacturers and supporting new ventures within the industry. Strauss also served as mentor for the great toy manufacturer, Louis Marx, who purchased his dies and molds and continued to produce toys marked Strauss for Strauss's retail stores.

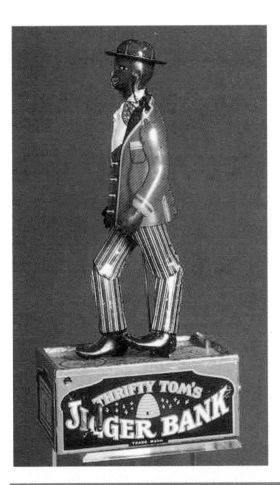

Above left: Thrifty Tom's Jigger Bank, patented in May 1910, is made of lithographed tin and features a clever clockwork mechanism that allows the figure to do a jig when it is activated by a deposited coin. **Top:** A lithographed tinplate toy, Alabama Coon Jigger features a clockwork mechanism that, when activated, causes the figure to dance. **Above:** This lithographed tinplate piano player and banjo player clockwork wind-up toy is known as Ham and Sam, Minstrel team. It is circa 1921. **Left:** This Circus Wagon is made of lithographed tin, and features a lion and lion tamer with front driver and colorful marquee. This toy also has a clockwork mechanism.

Structo Manufacturing Company
Freeport, Illinois
1908 - 1975

Above: This pair of streamlined pressed-steel Structo automotive toys features running boards and rubber tires.

Two brothers, Louis and Edward Strohacker of Freeport, Illinois, decided to create a toy manufacturing company that produced Structo Model Building Outfits, which were similar to the later Erector Sets. The brothers enlisted assistance from C.C. Thompson of Lowell, Massachusetts. The first three years of production proved to be quite successful. The building sets were very popular, however, in 1911 the English toy company Meccano slapped the Structo Company with an infringement of patent lawsuit.

For the next eight years the suit was in and out of the U.S. courts and finally was resolved with the court siding with Structo. Because Meccano wanted to dominate the Erector Set market, the company then purchased the patent rights and dies from the Structo Company. Ironically, Meccano merged with the A.C. Gilbert Company in 1919 to solely distribute Erector Sets in America.

By 1919, the Stutz Bearcat automobile skyrocketed to popularity and Structo was able to obtain the rights to produce toy versions of the designs. The line proved very popular and the next year the company came out with a truck and #8 racer. There was a wide variety of construction kits in a variety of sizes. In 1921 a #12 DeLuxe Auto was added to the line. The construction kit and ready-built toys produced during this time were priced between $3 to $11.

The depression years forced the company to be creative and come out with a line of push toys that were made of steel, very simple in design and affordable. This move helped keep the company afloat during a very difficult economic climate. The company continued to weather the stormy economic recovery, and developed new business arrangements with the A. C. Gilbert Company to distribute their toys.

In 1935 the Strohackers sold a major portion of the business to J. G. Gokey and divested themselves of the remainder in 1945. The company continued to produce toys and construction kits through the 1960's. It was acquired by Ertl in 1975.

Top: Structo's diverse line of pressed-steel toys included dump trucks as well as convertible coupe automobiles. **Above:** A pair of pressed-steel fire toys includes a pumping fire engine, featuring an orange water tank with brass hand pump mounted to the floor, left, and a hook and ladder truck with a hose reel, right. **Left:** The company also manufactured other utility vehicles, such as this truck.

Top: This pressed-steel fire truck has a nickel grill, open-body frame, water tank, hose reel and two side-mounted ladders. **Above:** This pressed-steel dump truck, left, has cast-iron spokes, a running board and clockwork mechanism. The Bear Cat roadster, right, has disc wheels, floorboards and a clockwork mechanism. **Right:** Structo advertised its toys in the December 1927 issue of *Child Life*, right, and the May 1928 issue, far right.

Tinkertoys
Evanston, Illinois
1915

Inspiration hit Charles Pajeau, an Evanston, Illinois, tombstone cutter, as he watched children play with wooden thread spools and knitting needles. He borrowed the design and concept of the circular shape of the knitting needles and the holes of the spool, adding more holes to give multiple options of stick placement and multiple design possibilities. He tinkered with his invention for two years before presenting his prototype at the New York Toy Fair in 1915. Being a novice to the toy industry, Pajeau was assigned to a table placed in the far corner of the hall, and didn't make a single sale.

Returning to Illinois by train, Pajeau walked into Grand Central Terminal and, in one last desperate attempt to make a sale, convinced two drugstores in the terminal to carry his creation in exchange for forty cents on every dollar sold. From this simple beginning, Pajeau created an elaborate window display consisting of various creations made with his Tinkertoys. He assembled an elaborate windmill and positioned a fan nearby to give his creation mobility. He also hired men to sit in the windows demonstrating the ease of multiple structures and construction possibilities. Crowds gathered and sales skyrocketed. A similar window display was arranged at a Philadelphia department store, resulting in more than nine hundred thousand sets sold. Since Pajeau walked into that drugstore in Grand Central Terminal, close to two hundred million sets of Tinkertoys have been sold.

Identification Clues

- Look for the Tinkertoys logo and the trademark circular canister

- Since these toys were mass-produced and are readily available, they have little secondary market value

Above: The broad range of construction options possible with Tinkertoys was advertised in issues of *Child Life* magazine dating, from left, November 1928, November 1927 and December 1927.

Tootsietoy
Chicago, Illinois
1876 - 1961

Identification Clues

- Look for the company logo on the piece, which is usually on the bottom or underside of the toy

  TOOTSIETOY
  MADE IN
  USA

- Small colorful cast-metal pieces of cast metal. Zinc replaced lead in the mid 1930s. The earlier lead pieces are heavier, so a piece's weight can help date it.

Above: Room settings produced by Tootsietoy consisted of lithographed tin-plate walls and metal accessories in each room.

This company has publishing in its ancestry, and can be credited with creating some of the earliest premium, or gift-with-purchase, concepts. The Dowst Brothers Company, a publishing company, first produced and distributed the National Laundry Journal in 1876. In 1893 Samuel Dowst attended the Colombian Exhibition and spotted a typecasting machine, the linotype, which produced small buttons or pins. The Dowst brothers decided the machine could produce small novelty items, which they could offer as premiums for their magazine. They started by producing political give-aways and lead collar buttons.

By the turn of the century, The Dowst Company began to realize how popular the premium market was with the public. In order to meet that demand they needed to expand the line of items offered, but where would the next great idea come from? They focused on the changing landscape of American industry and, in 1906, they had a great success with a miniature version of a Ford Model T. Over fifty million of these toys were sold. The Dowsts went on to create a variety of other vehicles, including a limousine with free-turning wheels, a Ford tour-ing car, and a matching Ford pick up truck.

Recognizing the popularity of these toys, the company continued to look for new pieces to meet the public demand. In 1922, Dowst introduced a line of metal doll furniture, naming it Tootsietoy, after Toots, the grand-daughter of one of the brothers. Soon Tootsietoy became the name of the entire toy division of Dowst.

In 1926 the parent company merged with Cosmo Manufacturing Company and became known as the Dowst Manufacturing Company. The Depression of the 1930s placed a huge financial burden on the company, however, they pulled together all their resources to streamline production and keep costs at a minimum. The overall attractiveness and low price range continued to make the toys a huge success around the country. The Tootsietoy Speedway, Airport set and variety of car designs continued to feed the public's hunger for new toy designs. The Dowsts even ventured into the science-fiction realm by producing a set of Buck Rogers Spacecrafts named Flash Blast Attack ship and Venus Duo-Destroyer.

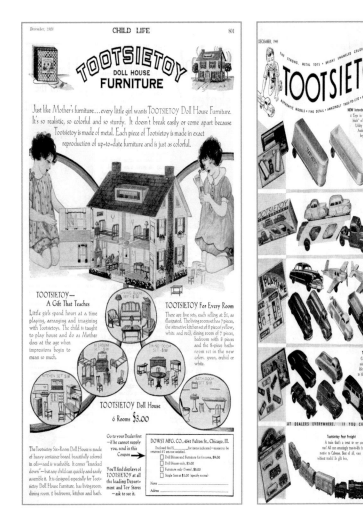

Collector Alert

Look out for repainting or chipped paint on collectibles. This will significantly reduce the value of the piece. If the paint looks wet or very bright, the chances are greater that the toy is not original.

Far left and left: Dowst advertised its wide-ranging variety of Tootsietoys over several decades. The advertisement for the dollhouse and furniture was published in *Child Life* magazine in December 1928, while the vehicles were featured more than twenty years later, in a December 1949 issue of the same magazine.

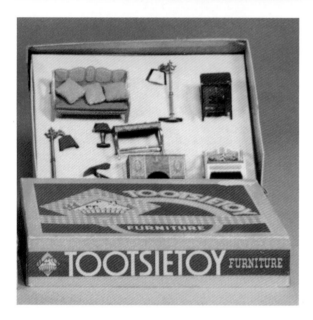

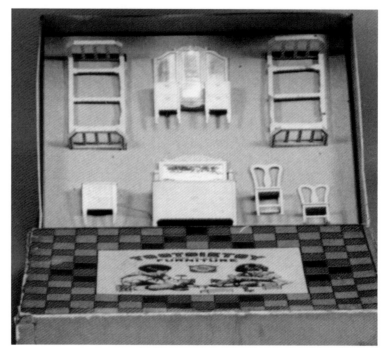

Above and right: The quality and variety in the Tootsietoy line are evident from the graphics on the boxtops to the die-cut wheels inside the box. The toys shown here all date from the 1930s.

Izannah Walker
Central Falls, Rhode Island
1873 - 1880s(?)

Very few dolls made by this mysterious nineteenth-century woman still survive, but those that do are so distinctive and prized that research continues to be done into her work. While doll scholars strongly suspect that she was making dolls prior to 1873, this is the date of her United States patent. Genealogical research has uncovered that she was born on September 25, 1817, in Rhode Island and lived in that state in the 1860s, '70s and '80s. Her cloth dolls, which typically stand approximately 16-19 inches high, are primitive in style, with stockinet and cotton batting over hand-pressed cloth, all hand painted in oil with minimal brush strokes. The cloth torsos are covered with polished cotton; the fingers are independently outlined, but sewn together, except for the thumb, which is separated. Earlier dolls had individually stitched toes, but later ones include painted-on shoes. The joints are sewn at the shoulders and hips. The painted hairstyles are very short and often boylike, although some styles have definite curls in front of the ears. The painted face, always with a closed mouth, bears an engimatic half smile, or sometimes a decidedly unsmiling expression.

Because of the materials used in their construction, Izannah Walker dolls are rarely found in mint condition. Still, they are highly valued examples of American folk art, and are among the rarest and most valuable American dolls today.

Identification Clues
- While most dolls are unmarked, the distinctive primitive style is instantly recognizable
- Occasionally a doll is marked: Patented Nov. 4, 1873 on the back of its head

Collector Alert
It is nearly unheard of to find an Izannah Walker doll in mint condition, so expect some paint wear and crazing. A repainted Izannah Walker doll is very undesirable.

Above: This 19 ½-inch high example of a cloth doll by Izannah Walker is in very good condition. Note the fine painting of the facial features and the hairstyle as well as the individually outlined fingers, which are sewn together, with a separated thumb.

Weeden Manufacturing Company
New Bedford, Massachusetts
1877 - 1939

Identification Clues

- Look for company name on toys
- Search out positive examples since some toys may not be marked

Above: The extremely rare mechanical bank called Ding Dong Bell was patented in August 1888. Made of tin with a wooden back panel, the bank depicts children at play. When the mechanism is wound and a coin placed in the slot, the boy seated on the fence begins to wave his hat while the others swing the bell next to the boy attempting to pull a cat from the well. **Above right:** Weeden's tin Plantation Darkey Savings Bank was patented in August 1888. When the clockwork mechanism is activated, the figures begin to perform their song and dance routine and the coin is deposited.

As a youngster, William N. Weeden worked as an apprentice in the watch and jewelry trade. He was fascinated by the intricacies and precision of the watch mechanisms and looked for ways to perfect the craftsmanship. He eventually founded his company in the town that was his birthplace.

Some early Weeden products include a simple pocket tin matchbox, magic lanterns, mechanical banks, and a pocket watchcase complete with music mechanism. The company was successful, and in 1884 Weeden teamed up with the publishers of *Youth's Companion* magazine to offer a premium toy to young boys who sold subscriptions of the magazine. The toy was an inexpensive and workable steam engine. The first year alone he produced more than ten thousand steam engines. The upright engine was patented in 1885 and was used by the magazine for many years after.

The company seemed to have found the niche Weeden was looking for. The steam engines became quite popular and the company responded by producing twenty-four various designs. Through the late 1800s the company experienced several re-organizations, but the toy production continued to increase, expanding to include steam-powered boats, trains and a fire engine with a working pumper. The manufacturer also discovered an entire market devoted to accessories to be used in conjunction with the steam engines. By 1922, Weeden reported more than one hundred different toys in their line for that year. The *Ladies Home Journal* and *New Styles* offered Weeden toys as premiums for subscribing to their magazines.

By the end of the 1920s Weeden was experiencing financial trouble, and could not hold on through the depression years. The company was sold to the Pairpoint Company in the early 1930s; however this company was also unable to make a profit with the toy division and discontinued the Weeden toys in 1939.

Boy's Steam Engine

Given for Five Subscriptions

WITH steam up and wheel a-turning, a boy has a toy that can't fail to amuse and instruct. The Weeden engine, shown here, is one of the most powerful toy engines made. It is modeled after the common "donkey" engines and has fly-wheel with pulley, safety-valves, whistle, shutoff, and glass water-gauge to indicate the amount of water in the boiler. It stands 9 inches high and is designed for running such toy machinery as a buzz-saw, tackle, etc. Many principles of engineering are thus taught in a practical way which may easily develop, in the young mind, a taste for a life's vocation. Each engine is thoroughly tested and fully warranted. Full directions for operating are included. When ordering please mention **Gift No. 6409.**

1900

Weeden's Double Mill Engine.

This superior Engine is the outcome of a desire for Steam Power of greater strength. It has two Boilers, both supplying steam to the two Cylinders. These Cylinders and their Steam Chests, Slide - Valves, Eccentrics and Rods are similar to those of the Single Engine shown below. The Fly-Wheel is heavy, 3½ inches in diameter. Has no dead centre. Size of base 9½ x 7 in.

A miniature factory or mill, constructed of thin board and fitted with toy machinery, run by this Engine, makes a striking window attraction. Any enterprising merchant would hire it.

Weight 4 lbs.

All "brick-work," including the tall chimney, —10 inches high,— is painted in a realistic manner. Other parts are in black and gold. Its power is ample for running a toy factory.

Above left: A May 1924 advertisement illustrated and described in detail the live steam engine shown at top. The engine educated children about how steam energy was created. **Above:** An advertisement in the July 1902 issue of *Little Folks* featured a variety of items made by Weeden, while a page in the company's 1900 catalog showcased the Double Mill Engine, left.

Wilkins Toy Company
Keene, New Hampshire
1880 - 1919

Identification Clues

- Cast-iron transportation toys
- Carpet toys like trains, paddle boats and horse-drawn vehicles
- Wilkins autos have vulcanized rubber wheels

James S. Wilkins founded the Triumph Wringer Company and first produced toy washing machines and locomotives made from cast-iron. Ten years later, Wilkins had acquired several patents for toy designs and acted primarily as a jobber with other toy manufacturers of the time. He changed the name of the company to the Wilkins Toy Company. His first line of toys consisted of trains; horse-drawn carriages; carts; and cast iron wagons; followed by auto-aerial ladder trucks; fire engines; autos; trucks; and racers.

The vehicles he produced ranged from seven to eighteen inches long and were powered by a long running flat-spring mechanical motor mounted horizontally at the rear of the toy. Financial trouble led him to accept the offer of Harry Thayer Kingsbury to purchase the company in 1895, however the Wilkins name was used on the toys through the end of the First World War. In 1919 the firm became known as the Kingsbury Toy Company, which continue to make toys until the outbreak of World War II.

Top: This simple Wilkins design features a horse-drawn cart with driver. **Above:** This cast-iron locomotive, tender and two cars set is representative of the type of trains the company produced. **Right:** The "City of New York" cast-iron paddle-wheel boat has red trim and a black smoke stack and two decks. Its articulated action is supported by three wheels for pulling.

Wolverine Supply & Manufacturing
Pittsburgh, Pennsylvania
1903 - 1950s

This company first started by manufacturing tin novelties that ranged in price from 5 to 25 cents, and took America by storm. Products were in demand and the company continued to grow to the point that in 1915 a three-story fireproof factory was built on Page Street in Pittsburgh with more than forty thousand square feet of space.

The early toys of the company relied on the weight of marbles or sand to set the toys in motion. The motion of the toy continued unattended until the supply was depleted. The highly colorful lithography coupled with the action made the toys very popular. Wolverine then expanded the line to include windmill toys that operated in the same manner, providing hours of entertainment for children. Wolverine called these types of toys "Sandy Andy" Automatic toys.

In March 1918, at the Toy Fair in New York City, Wolverine broke with its tradition and introduced a line of toys focusing on girls. Included were tea sets; sand pails; washtubs; glass washboards; ironing boards; and miniature grocery stores. As the toy line continued to expand in growth and popularity, so did the facilities used to make the popular toys. The company built an additional five-story factory to keep up with consumer demands.

By the mid 1920s Wolverine had established itself as a major supplier of toys for both girls and boys. Popular toys from this decade include the "Sandy Andy Dancing Doll" and the "Over-and-Under" mechanical racecar toy. These simple toys were children's favorites, and by the end of 1930 the Wolverine company had expanded its production facilities to 93,000 square feet, solely committed to the manufacturing of toys. The firm foundation the company established from the start, and its ability to keep costs low, enabled Wolverine to withstand the Depression and to add airplanes, boats, busses and other transportation toys to the line. Wolverine continued making toys through the 1950s.

Identification Clues
- Look for the company logo
- Look for the "Wolverine" name somewhere on the toy
- Color lithography
- Simple design and simple action

Top left: Wolverine's colorful lithographed merry-go-round is complete with flags, horses and clockwork mechanism. **Top right:** Sandy Andy Rooster is a colorful lithgraphed pull toy. A rare piece, it is shown with its original box. **Above:** This lithographed tinplate zilotone toy has a clockwork mechanism.

Wyandotte Toys (All Metal Products Company)
Wyandotte, Michigan
1920 - 1956

The company that became known as Wyandotte was originally founded as the All Metal Products company by George Stallings and William F. Schmid, who intended to produce automobile parts but decided, instead, to manufacture toy guns and rifles. Over nine years the company expanded production to include: pressed-steel airplanes; miniature automobiles; racers; mechanical toys; musical tops; pressed-steel dustpans; basket trays; and other playhouse toys. In 1924 a fire destroyed the factory, but a new plant was quickly constructed to meet the demand for the growing line.

By 1935, Wyandotte reported it had distributed five million toy guns worldwide. The 1930s proved to be the most popular decade for this company. It was during this period that Wyandotte produced its large pressed-steel automobiles with fine enamel finish and battery-powered lights. The next two decades saw numerous management changes and reorganizations, as well as the purchase of the William Hafner company in 1950. When plastic toys became the rage in the mid-1950s, Wyandotte was not able to keep up with the changing technologies and filed for bankruptcy on November 6, 1956.

Above: Wyandotte's pressed-steel crane truck has rounded fenders, a front bumper and rubber tires. **Right:** This lithographed tinplate rabbit is riding a motorcycle with a sidecar. It has a clockwork mechanism.

Above: This pressed-steel cargo truck has teardrop-shaped fenders and rubber tires. Left: The colorful lithographed tin Humphrey mobile, shown with its original box. features the rotund comic character riding an outhouse-shaped bike.

REFERENCE

I. Aids to Toy Identification

While it is often difficult to identify the makers of older toys that are not clearly marked, there are numerous ways to identify a toy's general time period and geographical origin. Familiarizing yourself with the various materials, types of vehicles and types of mechanisms, as well as the patent numbers for American toys made after 1860 can help you narrow down the possible makers. This section of the book will provide some general information that should help you learn more about your toy.

A. Materials

• **Wooden** toys, decorated or not, represent the oldest mass-produced category of toy production, dating back to around 1855 in the United States, and much earlier in Germany and other countries. The earliest decorated wooden toys were hand painted, and have a homemade appearance. In the mid-nineteenth century, stenciling was introduced, in which a brass template with a cut-out design was placed on the wooden surface. Paint was applied to the cut-out areas to create the design on the toy. Sometimes printed designs were impressed directly onto the wood. Late in the nineteenth century, after 1875, color lithography was the most common form of decoration for wooden toys. The designs could be printed directly onto the toys, or the lithographed paper would be glued onto them.

• **Cast-iron** toys were made in America beginning after the Civil War through World War II, when most production moved overseas. When the Civil War ended in 1865, many foundries that had been manufacturing guns, ammunition and supplies devoted themselves solely to meeting the great demand for toys by producing cast-iron playthings. (European manufacturers also made cast-iron toys but could not compete with the quality or quantity of toys made in America's numerous foundries.) The production process was simple. A wood-carved pattern was pressed into a sand-and-clay mixture, then removed, leaving a cavity that was filled with molten brass or bronze, which cooled and created the pattern. This rough casting was cleaned up to become the master pattern mold for the cast-iron toys. Hot molten iron was poured into the molds and allowed to cool. The molds could be used over and over again, making the process ideal for mass-production. The toys were cleaned up, hand painted and boxed for delivery. Reproduction cast-iron toys are easily identified by the grainy and bumpy appearance of the casting as well as by the uneven edges.

• **Tinplate** toys were first produced in America during the 1840s, when one of the first tin ore mines opened in Galena, Illinois, sparking the domestic production of tin products and decreasing the need to rely on imported tin. Tin toys were produced in larger quantities around 1880 through the early part of the 1900s, while mass-production of tinplate wind-up spring-driven toys dominated the first forty years of the twentieth century. Once World War II began, the scarcity of materials and rationing for the war efforts brought an end to tinplate-toy production in America. Japan, Korea and China took over the manufacturing of tin toys until the 1970s when plastic-toy production became prevalent.

• **Pressed steel** was used to make certain elements of toys prior to the twentieth century. It was not until the 1900s that toy companies utilized the material for the production of the entire toy. Companies like Buddy L and Keystone used heavy-gauge pressed steel to make riding toys and oversized trucks and cars. In the 1960s Tonka was the last company to utilize the pressed steel in the production of its toys before changing over to plastic in the 1970s.

• **Composition** toys are a mixture of materials—wood shavings, sawdust, plaster, cloth and wood pulp—combined and molded into shapes and figures that were painted or decorated after they dried. These toys look like wood, but are much more fragile, and deteriorate in dry, arid conditions. Composition was used primarily from around 1910 to 1940 for dolls' bodies and limbs as well as for character figures, military figures and small novelty toys.

• **Celluloid** is a highly flammable form of plastic that was invented in the United States in the late 1860s by the Hyatt brothers. It was used to simulate ivory in the early 1900s and was popular for toymaking during the 1920s through the 1950s. The original chemical trade name for celluloid was Pyroxylin. The material is extremely fragile, and celluloid toys in good condition are very desirable to collectors.

• **Plastic**, a synthetic material that is pliable and easy to mold when soft and hardens when left to set, was introduced into toy production in the late 1940s and became the primary material for toys by the 1970s.

B. Vehicle Descriptions:

Horse-drawn toys were based upon original life-size vehicles of the 1880s and 1890s, such as the following.

- **Barouche:** An open four-wheeled rig with the driver's seat elevated in front, and two seats facing each other.
- **Brake:** An open, sporting, four-wheeled rig that may seat two or three people.
- **Brougham:** An elegant, closed four-wheeled carriage with the driver's seat on the exterior. It was named after Lord Henry Brougham, Scottish Leader of House of Commons from 1830 to 1840.

- **Gig**: An open, sporting, two-wheeled vehicle, high off the ground, which was often used to exercise trotting horses.
- **Hansom Cab**: A popular, covered two-wheeler used to transport one or two passengers. The driver controlled the reins from a platform at the rear of the cab.
- **Landau**: A four-wheeled carriage with a divided top that could be thrown back or let down and a raised seat for the driver.
- **Phaeton**: An elegant, open four-wheeled carriage; later a type of touring car.
- **Tally-ho**: An open four-wheeled rig that could carry as many as twelve passengers inside and atop the vehicle.

C. Toy Mechanisms

- **Live Steam** is usually found in boats and early locomotives. A simple brass boiler is heated externally by a spirit lamp, generating steam power for a single or twin cylinder engine.
- **Clockwork** toys are powered by springs of various sizes that are wound. Depending on the mechanism's complexity, it will power the toy for at least a few minutes. Sophisticated early American clockwork toys could run for as long as thirty minutes.
- **Electric Motors** in earlier toys made use of alternating currents, which were poorly insulated and potentially lethal if short circuited. These were popular until low voltage systems became prevalent in the 1930s.
- **Lightweight Electric Mechanisms** were popular in toys that were made in Japan after 1945. The batteries are stored in the base of the toy or in a control panel.
- **Friction Motors** consist of a free-spinning laminated iron disc that powers the toy when the disc is spinning.

D. Toy Markings

The markings on toys provide collectors with valuable information and insight into the time period of production. Any product, including toys, made after 1891 and imported into the United States, had to be marked with the country of origin before the item was allowed into the country. Some companies only provided the necessary markings on the box, packaging or on tags, rather than permanently marking the toy itself. We have President McKinley and his Tariff Act of 1891 to thank for providing collectors with some clues as to the origin of toys made after 1891 and throughout the twentieth century.

Japanese Markings

After World War II, from 1945-1952, the United States occupied Japan and assisted with the rebuilding of the country's economy, including the production of novelties, ceramic pieces and toys. Items made during that period were required to be marked "Occupied Japan" to satisfy the export requirements. On April 28, 1952 , the sanction was lifted and the occupation by the United States ended. Because of the relatively short production time period of this marking requirement, "Made in Occupied Japan" items have become a favorite with collectors. Items made in Japan prior to the Second World War are usually marked "Japan," and those made after the occupation of Japan are marked "Made in Japan".

To complicate matters, certain items that were made during the occupied period may only be marked "Japan," while the box is marked "Occupied Japan. " This is the case with toys that were already in production prior to the occupation. In these cases, the box or crate in which the toys were shipped was the only thing marked "Occupied Japan." These markings might appear on playthings such as celluloid wind-up toys, plush-covered tin wind-up animals and tin wind-up vehicle toys.

German Markings

Prior to World War II, toys that were exported into the Untied States did list the country of origin as mandated, but also sometimes included the abbreviation "D. R. G. M.," or "Deutsches Reichsgebrauchsmuster," which indicated that the toy had a German registered patent for the item. After World War II, the United States occupied Germany, and from 1947-1953 exported items had to be marked: "U.S. Zone Germany." In 1949 toys began to be marked with the words: "Made in Western Germany." This marking continued through the 1960s. Examples of all three of these marks can be found on Schuco wind-up toys; the white tags marked U. S. Zone can be found on Steiff bears and animals.

E. Patent Numbers

One way to date a toy is to check if the United States Patent Numbers are available. But remember: just because a patent was issued in a certain year doesn't necessarily mean the toy was made in that year. **The year the patent was issued indicates the earliest possible year the toy may have been made.** Use the patent date and key on the following pages to help estimate the time period of a toy.

A Key To Patent Dates

Year	Patent Number
1860	26,642
1861	31,005
1862	34,045
1863	37,266
1864	41,047
1865	45,685
1866	51,784
1867	60,658
1868	72,959
1869	85,503
1870	93,460
1871	110,617
1872	122,304
1873	134,504
1874	146,120
1875	158,350
1876	171,641
1877	185,813
1878	198,733
1879	211,078
1880	223,211
1881	236,137
1882	251,685
1883	269,820
1884	291,016
1885	310,163
1886	333,494
1887	355,291
1888	375,720
1889	395,305
1890	418,665
1891	443,987
1892	466,315

Year	Patent Number
1893	488,976
1894	511,744
1895	531,619
1896	552,502
1897	574,369
1898	596,467
1899	616,871
1900	640,167
1901	664,827
1902	690,385
1903	717,521
1904	748,567
1905	778,834
1906	808,618
1907	839,799
1908	875,679
1909	908,436
1910	945,010
1911	980,178
1912	1,013,095
1913	1,049,326
1914	1,083,267
1915	1,123,212
1916	1,166,419
1917	1,210,389
1918	1,251,458
1919	1,290,027
1920	1,326,899
1921	1,364,063
1922	1,401,948
1923	1,440,362
1924	1,478,996
1925	1,521,590

Year	Patent Number
1926	1,568,040
1927	1,612,790
1928	1,654,521
1929	1,696,897
1930	1,742,181
1931	1,787,424
1932	1,839,190
1933	1,892,663
1934	1,944,449
1935	1,985,878
1936	2,026,510
1937	2,066,309
1938	2,101,004
1939	2,142,080
1940	2,185,170
1941	2,227,418
1942	2,268,540
1943	2,307,007
1944	2,338,081
1945	2,366,154
1946	2,391,856
1947	2,413,675
1948	2,433,824
1949	2,457,797
1950	2,492,944
1951	2,536,016
1952	2,580,379
1953	2,624,046
1954	2,664,562
1955	2,698,434
1956	2,728,913
1957	2,775,762
1958	2,818,567

Year	Patent Number
1959	2,866,973
1960	2,919,443
1961	2,966,681
1962	3,015,103
1963	3,070,801
1964	3,116,487
1965	3,163,865
1966	3,226,729
1967	3,295,143
1968	3,360,800
1969	3,419,907
1970	3,487,470
1971	3,551,909
1972	3,631,539
1973	3,707,729
1974	3,781,914
1975	3,858,241
1976	3,930,271
1977	4,000,520
1978	4,065,812
1979	4,131,952
1980	4,180,867
1981	4,242,757
1982	4,308,202
1983	4,366,579
1984	4,423,523
1985	4,490,885
1986	4,562,596
1987	4,663,526
1988	4,716,594
1989	4,794,652
1990	4,890,335

II. GLOSSARY

All-bisque — A doll made exclusively from bisque, usually no more than ten inches high.

Animated toy — Any plaything that simulates lifelike movements, whether powered or activated by spring, string, flywheel, rubber band, gravity, controlled movement of sand, gyroscopic mechanism, steam, electricity or batteries.

Applied ears — Ears made separately from a molded doll's head and applied later, rather than being part of the mold.

Articulated — The term describing a jointed toy with movable limbs.

Automaton (plural, automata) — A mechanical figure that is capable of performing multiple complex movements. Early examples feature doll-like bodies with composition or bisque heads.

Axel — A metal rod joining two vehicle or wagon wheels.

Balance toys – A motion toy that is counterweighted with pebbles, buckshot or another material in order to constantly return it to its starting position, such as a roly-poly toy. This term is also used for Early American tin toys that were weighted above or below the toy to maintain its equilibrium when it was set in motion.

Balance wheel — Most often seen on horse-drawn vehicles, this is a small rotating or stationary wheel normally attached to a front hoof, or a shaft suspended between two horses, which facilitates passage across the floor.

Ball joint — A ball-shaped joint joining a doll's limbs to its body.

Bébé — The French term for a doll representing a child rather than an adult.

Bisque — A malleable ceramic material with an unglazed surface used, among other things, in the manufacture of dolls' heads and limbs. Bisque can be poured into a mold or pressed into shape, before being fired at a high temperature.

Board games — Games played on a specially designed card or fabric surface. The most common types of games involve players moving across the board by throwing dice and using counters to mark their position on the board.

Carpet toy — A Victorian term for a toy meant to be played with on the carpets that covered the wooden floors in homes of that era.

Cast-iron toys — Made of molten gray high-carbon iron, hand-poured into sand-casting molds; usually cast in halves, then mated and bolted or riveted as one. More elaborate versions incorporated interlocking, nickel-plated grills, chassis, bumpers, people, and other accessories.

Celluloid — An early and highly flammable form of plastic used for making toys. Invented in the United States in 1869 by the Hyatt Brothers, its original chemical name is Pyroxylin.

Character doll — A doll with a realistic rather than idealized expression.

China — Glazed porcelain used, among other things, in the manufacture of dolls' heads.

Clockwork Mechanism — Made of machined brass and steel and used to animate toys for as long as thirty minutes as interlocking gears move to uncoil spring. Produced as a drive system for toys by clock makers beginning in 1862 and ending about thirty years later in the Northeastern United States.

Cloth doll — A doll made from fabric.

Composition – An inexpensive substance made from a combination of cloth, wood, wood pulp, plaster of Paris, glue and sawdust, used for making doll's heads, bodies and limbs, as well as other toys.

Crazing – A random pattern of fine cracks in the paint of a hand enameled toy – usually a sign that the paint is old, but can be copied by the finest restorers.

DEP – An abbreviation of the French "déposé" or the German "Deponiert" indicating a registered patent; used on French and German dolls and often appearing as an incised mark on the heads of bisque dolls.

Die-cast – A shape formed in a metal mold under pressure. Lead was initially used as the main ingredient, but was replaced in Britain in 1934 with mazac (a magnesium and zinc-based alloy) which was safer.

Disc joint – A joint made from a cardboard disc held in place by a metal pin; used to articulate soft toys and teddy bears.

D.R.G.M. – (Deutsches Reichsgebrauchsmuster) The German term for the official governmental roll of registered patents.

Embossed – Pressed decoration on tinplate, done by a hand- or steam-powered press.

Excelsior – A soft mixture of long, thin wood shavings used for stuffing teddy bears.

Fashion doll – A French lady doll, usually with a kid body and bisque head, dressed in fashionable attire.

Fixed eyes – Simple glass eyes that do not move, used on dolls and teddy bears.

Flirty eyes – Glass dolls' eyes that open, close and move from side to side.

Floor-runner – A carpet train or toy that is propelled along the floor by a hand movement.

Flywheel – A mechanism used in some toys before 1914, which operates on the inertia principle, with power provided by hand or by string.

Friction wheel – A central inertia wheel, also known as a fly-wheel, activated by a spring in the rear wheels that sets the toy in motion. American toys utilized a cast-iron friction wheel; Europeans used cast lead. Friction toys were popular from 1900 to the early 1930s.

Growler – The voice box inside a teddy bear that produces a growling sound.

Impressed – The method whereby a maker's mark is indented into the surface of a toy, rather than raised.

Incised – The method whereby a maker's mark is scratched into the surface of a toy's head, rather than indented.

Inertia principle – The tendency of a body at rest to remain at rest, or of a body in motion to stay in motion, unless disturbed by an external force.

Intaglio eyes – Painted eyes with concave pupils and irises, carved into a bisque head.

Kapok – An extremely lightweight fiber used for stuffing teddy bears, sometimes in combination with other materials.

Kid – Soft leather used to make dolls' bodies, generally with bisque heads, during the nineteenth century.

Lead – A main ingredient in some die-cast toys until 1934; most widely used in making toy figures until the 1960s.

Licensing — The process whereby manufacturers pay for the rights to produce toys featuring characters or stories created by other companies or individuals. The characters are often of film, television or comic-strip fame.

Lithography — A printing process in which the image is scratched onto a stone or metal plate that is ink-repellent. When the plate is inked, the image alone prints onto the surface of paper, wood or tin. In the process of making tin toys, the sheets of tinplate are printed on the flat tin before being pressed into shapes.

Mazac — A magnesium-and-zinc-based metal alloy regularly used in the die-cast technique from 1934 onwards.

Mechanical bank — A savings box in which the depositing of coins depends on some mechanical action, usually made from cast-iron. These were particularly popular with both children and adults in the United States in the late nineteenth century, from about 1860 onwards.

Marriage — The term used to describe a toy or doll made from pieces that did not originally belong together.

Mohair — A fabric woven from the silky fleece of an angora goat and commonly used for making teddy bears.

Molded ears — Ears cast as an intrinsic part of the head mold of a doll.

Molded hair — Hair cast as an intrinsic part of the head mold of a doll.

Mold number — The recorded number of the mold used in the production of a bisque-headed doll, indicated by the numbers or letters impressed on the head.

Nickel-plating — The technique for coating cast-iron or steel toys with molten nickel to prevent rusting and enhance appearance.

Open-closed mouth — A type of doll's mouth that appears to be open but has no actual opening between the lips.

Open head — The term for the open-crowned head covered with a pate (usually cork or cardboard) to which a wig is attached, found on most bisque dolls.

Open mouth — A type of doll's mouth in which the lips are actually parted, sometimes with teeth showing.

Paperweight eyes — Realistic blown-glass eyes with white threads running through the irises, giving an impression of depth; also known as spiral glass eyes.

Papier-mâché — A combination of molded paper pulp, a whitening agent and glue, used during the nineteenth century for the construction of dolls' heads and bodies, and even full-scale furniture.

Pate — A crown piece found under the wig that covers the hole in some dolls' heads; made from cardboard, cork or plaster.

Patent — The exclusive right to manufacture a particular item. The stamp "Pat" or "Patd" appears on English and American toys.

Patent date — The date a maker received the exclusive right, indicated by a patent number, to manufacture an item. A patent number can help date an American toy made after 1860, or a German toy made after 1890.

Penny Toys — Inexpensive toys usually made from lithographed tinplate, with a simple push-along action. Production of these was primarily between 1900 and the 1930s.

Plastic — A synthetic material with a polymeric structure, which can be easily molded when soft, and then set. Plastic increasingly replaced tinplate as the primary material with which to make toys from the late 1940s onwards.

Plywood — A type of inexpensive laminate sometimes used to make wooden toys.

Porcelain — A fine-grained white ceramic ware, usually translucent, fired at high temperature and used for making dolls' heads and limbs, among other things.

Provenance — The documented history of ownership of any antique item. An unusual or notable provenance may enhance the value of a piece.

Reproduction — An exact copy of an antique object.

Rod bear — An early type of Steiff teddy bear with metal rod jointing.

S.F.B.J. — Initials of the Société Française de Fabrication des Bébés et Jouets, an association of French doll makers formed at the end of the nineteenth century in response to German competition.

Shoe-button eyes — Black wooden eyes with metal loops on the back, used on early teddy bears.

Shoulder head — The term for a doll's head and shoulders molded in one piece.

Shoulder plate — The area of a doll's shoulder-head below the neck.

Sleep eyes — Glass eyes that are open when the doll is upright and closed when the doll is laid horizontally.

Solid-domed head — A socket or shoulder-plate bisque doll's head with a solid crown made from bisque.

Socket head — A swivel head with a rounded base to the neck that enables the head to fit snugly into a cup shape at the top of a composition body.

Still bank — A savings bank that has no mechanical movement involved in the deposit of coins into it.

Stockinet — A soft cotton fabric sometimes used for doll bodies and occasionally for doll heads.

Swivel head — A doll's head made separately from the shoulder plate and fitted later, allowing the head to swivel.

Tabs — The method of joining two pieces of metal by folding a small tab through a slot.

Tinplate — Thin sheets of iron or steel that are coated with a tin-based alloy.

Turned — A term used to describe a wooden toy that has been shaped on a lathe.

Vinyl — A non-flammable, flexible yet tough plastic used for making dolls in the second half of the twentieth century.

Wind-ups — A term used interchangeably for both clockwork and spring-driven toys that must be wound to be activated.

III. BIBLIOGRAPHY

Bach, Jean. *Dictionary of Doll Marks*, New York, New York: Sterling Publishing Co., Inc., 1990.

Beckett, Alison. *Collecting Teddy Bears & Dolls-The Facts At Your Fingertips*, Great Britain: Reed International Books Limited, 1996.

Bristol, Olivia. *Dolls, A Collector's Guide*, Great Britain: De Agostini Editions, 1997.

Brooks, Jacki. *The Complete Encyclopedia of Teddy Bears*, Cumberland, Maryland: Hobby House Press, Inc., 1990.

Cieslik, Jurgen and Marianne. *Button In Ear*, Germany: Satz and Druck GMBH, 1989.

Cieslik, Jurgen and Marianne. *Steiff-Teddy Bears, Love For A Lifetime*, Germany: Druckhaus B. Kuhlen KG, Monchengladbach, 1994.

Cockrill, Pauline, *The Ultimate Teddy Bear Encyclopedia*, New York, New York: Dorling Kindersley, 1993.

Coleman, Dorothy, Evelyn Jane and Elizabeth Ann. *The Collector's Enyclopedia of Dolls, Volumes 1 and 2*, New York, New York: Crown Publishers, Inc., 1968 and 1986.

Foulke, Jan. *14th Blue Book of Dolls & Values*, Grantsville, Maryland: Hobby House Press, Inc., 1999.

Freed, Joe and Sharon. *Collector's Guide to American Transportation Toys*, Raleigh, North Carolina: Freedom Publishing Company, Inc. 1995.

Friz, Richard. *TOYS*, New York, New York: Random House, Inc. 1990.

Gardiner, Gordon and Alistair Morris. *The Illustrated Encyclopedia of Metal Toys*, Avenel, New Jersey: Random House Value Publishing, Inc. 1984.

Goddu, Krystyna Poray. *A Celebration of Steiff: Timeless Toys for Today*, New York, New York: Portfolio Press Corporation, 1997.

Heide, Robert and John Gilman. *The Mickey Mouse Watch*, Singapore: Disney Enterprises, Inc., 1997.

Hillier, Mary. *Pageant of Toys*, New York, New York: Taplinger, 1966.

Hockenberry, Dee. *The Big BEAR Book*, Atglen, Pennsylvania: Schiffer Publishing, Ltd., 1996.

Hockenberry, Dee. *Enchanting Friends*, Atglen, Pennsylvania: Schiffer Publishing Ltd., 1995.

King, Constance. *The Century of the Teddy Bear*, Woodbridge, Suffolk: Antique Collectors' Club Ltd., 1997.

Korbeck, Sharon. *1998 Toys & Prices*, Iola, Wisconsin: Krause Publications, Inc., 1997.

Mandel, Margaret Fox. *Teddy Bears & Steiff Animals*, Paducah, Kentucky: Collector Books, 1984.

Miller, Judith and Martin. *Miller's Toys and Games Antiques Checklist*, Great Britain: Reed Consumer Books Limited, 1995.

Mullins, Linda. *American Teddy Bear Encyclopedia*, Grantsville, Maryland: Hobby House Press, 1995.

Mullins, Linda. *The Teddy Bear Men*, Cumberland, Maryland: Hobby House Press, Inc., 1987.

Mullins, Linda. *4th Teddy Bear & Friends Price Guide*, Grantsville, Maryland: Hobby House Press, Inc., 1993.

Murray, John J. and Bruce R. Fox. *Fisher-Price, A Historical, Rarity, Value Guide*, Florence, Alabama: Books Americana, Inc., 1991.

O'Brien, Richard. *The Story of American Toys*, New York, New York: Cross River Press, Ltd. 1990.

O'Brien, Richard. *Collecting Toy Trains Identification and Value Guide*, Iola, Wisconsin: Krause Publications, 1997.

O'Brien, Richard. *Collecting Toys Identification and Value Guide*, Iola, Wisconsin: Krause Publications, 1997.

Reinelt, Sabine. *Kathe Kruse – Die Fruhen Jahre*, Duisburg: Verlag Puppen Und Spielzeug, 1994.

Richter, Lydia. *The Beloved Kathe Kruse Dolls, Yesterday and Today*, Cumberland, Maryland: Hobby House Press, Inc., 1991.

Rinehart, Joyce Gerardi. *Wonderful Raggedy Anns with Values*, Atglen, Pennsylvania: Schiffer Publishing Ltd., 1997.

Stanford, Maureen and Amanda O'Neill. *The Teddy Bear Book*, North Dighton, Massachussets: JG Press, 1995.

Whitton, Blair. *The Knopf Collectors' Guides to American Antiques: Toys*, New York, New York: Chanticleer Press, Inc., 1984.

Photo Credits

The publishers would like to acknowledge and thank the following individuals and organizations for the loan of photography for use in this book.

Jeanie Bertoia of Bertoia Auctions
2441 Demarco Dr.
Vineland, NJ 08360
856-692-1881
www.Bertoiaauctions.com
Page 27, all photos: Althof, Bergman and Company
Page 28, top: American Flyer
Page 29, bottom: American Flyer
Page 30, top and bottom: Arcade
Pages 31-33, all photos: Arcade
Page 35, top: Bing
Page 36, all photos: Bing
Page 37, top and bottom: Bing
Pages 38-39, all photos: Bliss
Page 40, all photos: Borgfeldt
Page 41, top left, all right: Borgfeldt
Pages 42-43, all photos: Bradley
Pages 44-48, all photos: Britains
Page 48, all photos: Brown
Page 49, top three photos: Brown
Page 50, all photos: Bru
Page 51, all photos: Buddy L
Page 52, top: Buddy L
Page 53, top left, all right: Buddy L
Pages 54-55, all photos:
Page 56, top and bottom: Georges Carette et CIE
Page 57, all photos: Georges Carette et CIE
Page 63, all photos: Chein
Pages 64-67, all photos: Chein
Page 69, all photos: Charles Crandall
Page 74, top: Dean's Rag
Page 75, top: Dent
Page 79, top: Effanbee
Page 80, top: Effanbee
Pages 82-83, all photos: Fallows
Page 94, all photos: Gibbs
Page 95, top: Gilbert
Page 96, top: Gilbert
Page 98, top: Girard
Page 99, all photos: Girard
Pages 100-101, all photos: Gong Bell
Page 104, all photos: Hafner
Page 105: Handwerck
Page 108, all photos: Hill Brass Co.
Pages 111-114, all photos: Hubley
Page 115: Ideal
Page 118, top left and right: Ideal
Page 119, all photos: Ingersoll
Page 120, left: Ingersoll
Page 121, all photos: Ingersoll
Page 104, top and bottom: Ives
Page 122, top and bottom: Ives
Page 123, all photos: Ives
Pages 124-125, top and all left: Ives
Pages 126-127: Jumeau
Page 128, all photos: Kämmer & Reinhardt
Pages 129-131, all photos: Kenton
Page 132: Kestner
Page 133: bottom left and right: Kestner
Page 134, top: Keystone
Page 135, all photos: Keystone
Page 136, all photos: Keystone
Page 138, all photos: Kilgore
Page 139: Kingsbury
Page 140, top: Kingsbury
Page 148, all photos: Kyser & Rex
Pages 149-155, all photos: Lehmann
Pages 156-157, all photos: Lenci
Pages 159-162, all photos: Lionel
Page 163, top and bottom: Lionel
Page 164, top and all right: Lionel

Page 165, all photos: Lionel
Pages 166-167, all photos: McLoughlin
Pages 173-179, all photos: Marx
Page 181, center and bottom right: Meccano
Pages 183-184, all photos: Metalcraft
Page 188, all photos: Pratt & Letchworth
Page 189, all photos: WS Reed
Pages 190-195, all photos: Schoenhut
Page 197, all photos: Schuco
Page 198, top: Schuco
Page 200, all photos: Schuco
Page 201, all photos: Schuco
Page 202, bottom: Schuco
Page 203-206, all photos: Shepard Hardware
Page 207: Simon and Halbig
Pages 208-211, all photos: Steelcraft
Pages 219-223, all photos: J&E Stevens
Page 224: Strauss
Page 225, top: Strauss
Page 226-227, all photos: Structo
Pages 230-232, all photos: Tootsietoy
Page 234, all photos: Weeden
Page 236, all photos: Wilkins
Page 237, all photos: Wolverine
Pages 238-239, all photos: Wyandotte

Greg Strahm, Treasure Quest Auction Galleries
2581 Jupiter Park Dr., Suite E5
Jupiter, Florida 33458
1-888-741-0777
www.tqag.com
Page 22: center and bottom
Page 34, all photos: Barclay
Page 41, bottom left: Borgfeldt
Page 56, center: Georges Carette et CIE
Page 58, all bottom: Chad Valley
Page 59, top and all right: Chad Valley
Pages 60-61, all photos: Character
Pages 71-73, all photos: Daisy
Page 76, top: Dent
Page 78, all photos: Duncan
Pages 91-93, all photos: Georgene
Page 116, all photos: Ideal
Page 117, bottom: Ideal
Page 118, bottom left and right: Ideal
Page 120, right: Ingersoll
Page 144, bottom left: Knickerbocker
Pages 168-169, all photos: Manoil
Page 171, center: Märklin
Pages 186-187, all photos: Ohio Art
Page 196, all photos: Schuco
Page 199, all photos: Schuco
Page 202, top: Schuco
Page 214, bottom: Steiff
Pages 235, all photos: Weeden

Tim's Toy Times, Inc.
2281 Jupiter Park Drive. Suite E5
Jupiter, Florida 33458
561-741-7527
www.timluke.net
Pages 2, 5, 7, 10-11, 14, 15, 16, 20
Page 28, center: American Flyer
Page 29, top: American Flyer
Page 30, center: Arcade
Page 52, bottom: Buddy L
Page 53, bottom left: Buddy L
Page 58, top left: Chad Valley
Page 70. Jesse Crandall
Page 75, bottom: Dent
Page 76, bottom: Dent
Page 77, all photos: Dent
Pages 85-89, all photos: Fisher-Price
Page 90, all photos: Francis Field & Francis

Page 95, bottom: Gilbert
Page 96, bottom: Gilbert
Page 97, all photos: Gilbert
Pages 102-103, all photos: Gund
Page 106: Hermann
Page 107, all photos: Hermann
Page 122, center: Ives
Page 124, right: Ives
Page 134, bottom: Keystone
Page 137, all photos: Kiddie Car
Page 140, center and bottom:Kingsbury
Page 158, all photos: Lincoln Logs
Page 163, center: Lionel
Page 164, left: Lionel
Page 180, all photos: Meccano
Page 181, left and top right: Meccano
Page 185, right: Metalcraft
Page 198, bottom: Schuco
Page 212, Steiff
Page 214, top: Steiff
Page 215, bottom: Steiff
Page 216, bottom: Steiff
Page 217, bottom: Steiff
Page 228, bottom: Structo
Page 229, all photos: Tinkertoys
Pages 240-241
Page 242

Walter Pfeiffer Studios
Dublin, Ireland
Page 22, top left and right: Alexander
Pages 23-26, all photos: Alexander
Page 213: Steiff
Page 215, top: Steiff
Page 216, top: Steiff
Page 217, top: Steiff
Page 218, all photos: Steiff

McMasters Auction House
P.O. Box 1755
Cambridge, OH 43725
1-800-842-3526
Page 62: Chase
Page 81, all photos: Effanbee
Pages 110-111, all photos: E.I. Horsman
Page 133, top: Kestner

Noel Barrett Antiques & Auctions Ltd.
Carversville, PA 18913
Page 49, bottom: Brown
Page 170: Märklin
Page 171-172, top and bottom: Märklin

Courtesy of Mort and Evelyn Wood
Page 37, top and bottom right: Bing
Page 58, top right: Chad Valley

Courtesy of Donna McPherson
Page 59, bottom left: Chad Valley
Page 68: Chiltern (Collection of Barbara Smith)
Page 182, top left: Merrythought

Courtesy of Dee Hockenberry
Page 84, top right: Farnell
Page 117, top: Ideal

Courtesy of Knickerbocker Toy Company
Pages 141-143, all photos: Knickerbocker
Page 144, top and right: Knickerbocker

Courtesy of The Käthe Kruse Doll Company
Pages 145-147, all photos: Kruse

Courtesy of Karen Strickland (Rare Bears collection)
Page 182, top right: Merrythought

Courtesy of Adrienne Zinsser (Bears of Charlton Court collection)
Page 84 , top left: Farnell

Toys from American Childhood: 1845-1945